ENDORSEMENTS

How have you benefitted from the Lifetogether coaching programs and materials found in Small Group University?

"Brett's enthusiasm, encouragement, and expertise is helping us get a strong foundation for this new venture in the life of our church.
- Earl Wheatley, Senior Pastor, North Park Church, MS

"The program has become THE driving force in developing a successful pathway for significant spiritual growth."
- Mike Womble, Associate Pastor, Winter Park Baptist Church, NC

As a Small Group Pastor, this has helped me think more strategically about "…our small group ministry in relation to the mission and vision of our church. It has also challenged me personally to grow as a leader."
-Todd Cullen, Life Group Pastor, North Star Church

"Created a burning desire… to connect 100% of our church in discipleship groups."
- Randy Smyre, Associate Pastor, Crossroads Church of the Nazarene, PA

"Awesome ideas and insight as to the next step in moving our congregation towards 100% participation in community life."
- Rhonda Schroder, Small Group Director, Cornerstone Church, MI

"Will focus the vision for your small group ministry by giving you tested ideas and tools as well as new and fresh ideas from those who are in the trenches with you."
-Rob Warnel

"Within the first month has stimulated my thoughts, motivated my actions, filled me with new insights and challenged me to reach higher while depending more on God."
-Scott Roderick, Discipleship Pastor, First Christian, CA

"Took us to a whole new level of joyful terror by showing us how to implement "blow-it-up" Small Group strategies."
- Bruce Southerland, Pastor of Membership, Manchester Christian Church, NH

"Caused me to think outside the box of my personal paradigm. The strategies and interaction with peers is invaluable."
-Rex Raines, Pastor of Spiritual Formation, Crossroads Church, IL

BUILDINGLIFE**TOGETHER**

BUILDING LIFETOGETHER

Building a Healthy Small Group Ministry in Your Church

- BRETT EASTMAN -
President and Founder, Lifetogether

HELLO MY NAME IS

Katherine Gonzalez

Lifetogether Minstries
29801 Santa Margarita Pkwy. Ste 100
Rancho Santa Margarita, CA 92688
Brett@lifetogether.com

http://twitter.com/bretteastman1
Facebook.com/DoingLifeTogether

COPYRIGHT

lifetogether

Building Lifetogether
Copyright © 2002, 2005, 2011 by Brett Eastman

Requests for information should be addressed to
Lifetogether
29801 Santa Margarita Pkwy, Suite 100
RSM, CA, 92688

ISBN 978-0-9827022-8-4

Scripture quotations, unless otherwise indicated, are taken from the HOLY BIBLE, NEW INTERNATIONAL VERSION®. NIV®. Copyright 1973, 1978, and 1984 by International Bible Society. Used by permission of Zondervan Bible Publishing House. All rights reserved.

Scripture references marked The Message are taken from THE MESSAGE. Copyright © 1993, 1994, 1995, 1996, 2000, 2001, 2002, 2005. Used by permission of NavPress Publishing Company.

Book Design by Tommy Owen, Zoobuzz Media

Multiple photos by Tanya Kay Photography, TanyaKayPhoto.com

TABLE OF CONTENTS:

Endorsements	3
Welcome	9
Winning at Lifetogether	10
A 30 Day Reading Plan For Small Group Ministry Directors	13

SESSIONS

Session 1: How to Launch and Lead a Small Group Ministry in Your Church — 14
    Why Small Groups are a Big Deal
    Small Group Success Isn't Just for Mega Churches
    Imagine Connecting 25-50% of Your Congregation
    From Dream to Reality
    12 Steps in Planning Your Small Group Launch

Session 2: Connect your Entire Congregation into Community—Fellowship — 29
    Reconnecting The Connected
    Numbers Don't Matter
    Launching Community
    From Soloist To Choir
    Small Groups Built To Last

Session 3: Cultivate an Unlimited Number of Leaders to Reach Your Community for Christ—Evangelism — 36
    Five Strategies for Sustaining Momentum after Your Campaign
    No time, No Resources
    Small Groups Help Believers Fulfill the Great Commission Together
    Evangelism Explosion
    Put People into Ministry, Not on Committees

Session 4: Create Healthy & Balanced Groups that Grow Over Time—Service — 45
    Six Tips for Keeping New Small Groups Healthy
    Where Do We Go from Here?
    10 Ways to Sustain Your New Small Groups
    Coaching that Works
    Top 10 Learnings from a Lifetogether Summit

Session 5: Coach and Train Your Leaders for Life—Discipleship — 61
    Mentor your Coaches and Their Leaders
    Sometimes Ministry Is Messy
    Shaping Shepherds and Sheep
    Be a Champion to remember
    Coaching Life-Changing leaders

Session 6: Create a Culture that Celebrates Your Lifetogether—Worship — 70
    Build Community Through Communion
    Modeling the Heart of Celebration
    Top Seven List for the "Now What?" Moment
    Committed to Community
    Leadership Celebration

APPENDIX 82

Answer Key	83
Pastor FAQ's	84
Small Group Champion FAQ's	86
The Lifetogether Pathway	89
One Year of Purpose Goals	91
Host Orientation Agenda	92
Connecting Announcement Script	93
Small Group Coaching Ministry Description	95
Role of Community Leader	96
G.I.F.T.S. Profile Worksheet	98
Small Group Gift Development Table	99
Personal Health Assessment	100
Personal Health Plan	101
Small Group Health Assessment	102
Small Group Health Plan	103
Lifetogether Church Health Plan Example	104
Lifetogether Church Health Plan	105
Church Health Assessment	106
Small Group Leadership Lessons	107
Small Group Leadership 101	110
Great Conversation Starters	112

CASE STUDIES 113

A Tremendous gain	114
Connecting Everyone	116
Pushing the Pedal Down after 40 Days of Purpose	118
Discovering Community	121
The Power of 40 Days of Purpose	122
What a Ride!	124
When 100% Connected Falls Short of God's Plan	126
Small Church, Big on Groups	128
Making the Ask—Recruiting Hosts During a 30 Day Campaign	130
From 0 to 60 in Thirty Days	132
The Saddleback Story	134
How One Church Planted over 100 Purpose-Driven Churches	138
Beginning Lifetogether	140
Small Town—Big Impact	141
Connecting Everyone	143
A 'Blockbuster' Small Group Strategy	144
Rick Warren Foreword to Doing Lifetogether	147
Lifetogether Series	148
Small Group University	150
About the Author	151
Prayer and Praise Reports	153

WELCOME

Welcome to Small Group University,

You are about ready to follow the simple path that the twelve disciples took some two thousand years ago that ultimately transformed the world. Your simple step of faith may seem small now, but one day it could represent a link in the chain that will not only transform you life, your group and your church, but is sure to make a kingdom difference far greater than you could imagine. Small Group University provides you and your leaders a plug and play system to start and sustain healthy small groups based on the five biblical purposes. It is a breakthrough DVD and Companion 30-day study that helps "Build Leaders for Life." Whether you are a new small group host, an existing group leader, a coach of a few leaders or a small group ministry leader, you have come to the right place.

Small Group University is composed of four unique training series: Hosting Lifetogether, Coaching Lifetogether, and Building Lifetogether and creating Lifetogether. Hosting Lifetogether trains new leaders in gathering and leading their first group. Coaching Lifetogether gives practical training to your existing leaders and their groups. Building Lifetogether gives practical and proven support to pastors and small group directors in building and growing their small group ministry. Creating Lifetogether is a ten session series on how to host your own 40-Day campaign in your church. Best of all, it provides pastors with everything they need to launch and lead a healthy small group ministry in their churches in less than 90 days.

Hosting, Coaching and Building Lifetogether include a 30-day reading plan as a companion to the six-session DVD training series. The series can be viewed in a classroom setting all at once, followed by brief discussion times, studied over a period of time with a few leaders or even on your own as on online study. Either way you chose, a downloadable certificate of completion is available to anyone who completes each of the series. Simply go to Lifetogether.com when you're done and click "Small Group University," where you will also find many other downloadable small group resources.

As you begin, simply pray as Paul did to see God accomplish what is exceedingly, abundantly beyond whatever you would ask or think.

Blessings,

Brett Eastman
Founder and President, Lifetogether

WINNING IN LIFE TOGETHER
GOD'S PATHWAY FOR LIVING A LIFE OF PURPOSE.

In *The Purpose Driven Life*, Rick Warren writes, "God intends for us to experience life together. The Bible calls this fellowship … real fellowship is so much more than just showing up at services … It includes unselfish loving, honest sharing, practical serving, sacrificial giving, sympathetic comforting, and all the other 'one another' commands found in the New Testament."

I had to learn that truth the hard way.

My philosophy of life was primarily shaped by my life experience. I grew up in a single parent home with my two older sisters, a cousin, a widowed aunt, and my mom, who worked her fingers to the bone, trying to make ends meet. Since my mom worked around the clock and my father showed up once a year at Christmas, usually drunk, I was on my own most of the time. I defined my success by accomplishments, acquiring things, and making money.

"Even the Lone Ranger had Tonto," Warren writes in his book. But I didn't, which made me believe that if I was going to succeed in life, I would have to do it on my own strength. I didn't believe anyone else would be willing to help me—especially God.

One day, a girl I had been dating for several years told me she had found Jesus. Because of that event, my life took a significant turn.

Reluctantly, I decided to join a few guys who were doing a Bible study on the life of Christ. I'd never talked openly about the Bible, Jesus, and what it meant to have a relationship with him. Those five guys were so gracious with my cynical attitude, challenging questions, and fears about placing my trust in a God I couldn't see. They could imagine how scary it was to trust a heavenly father after growing up with a very distant and disappointing earthly father.

Through the lives of those men, I was ambushed by the love of God, and I no longer wanted to do life alone. I wanted what they had—a relationship with God and other believers.

That year, my girlfriend, who is now my wife of over 20 years, saw me give my heart and life over to the one who gave us life together.

From that point on, I was never the same. I redefined "winning in life." It wasn't about accomplishments, status, and money anymore, but about living a healthy and balanced life of purpose, best achieved by:

1. **Connecting** in life with a few friends and family on a deeper level than ever before in the context of a small group community (fellowship).

2. **Growing** in my spiritual journey through the encouragement and accountability of a few friends to help me be more like Christ (discipleship).

3. **Developing** my unique SHAPE for the purpose of ministry to others, not just my own selfish ambitions (ministry).

4. **Sharing** my life mission with others, because it's scary and difficult to do alone (evangelism).

5. **Surrendering** my heart to God and others for prayer and support as an act of worship to God (worship).

Grow and Go

After being in that group only a few months, my leaders asked if I would be willing to "grow and go" to the next level in my walk with God. He said, "You really don't know if you have it until you give it away."

He encouraged me to do as Jesus did—create my own circle of friends by asking God with whom he wanted me to connect and deciding with whom I would enjoy spending time for at least six weeks. He challenged me to call the few people God brought to mind, as a step of faith.

I was just crazy enough to do it—and the rest is history. Two of those men asked Christ into their lives, and several others became lifetime friends. One of them even stood as the best man in my wedding.

Maybe you're not in a group, but have been inspired by reading *The Purpose Driven Life*. You know that God wants you to be transformed by the purposes for life. This transformation process begins when you ask the question, "What am I going to do today with what He has revealed to me?"

Start by connecting with a few friends in a small group or establishing a spiritual partnership with a friend. Here is a simple ABC strategy to make your connection happen today.

Ask God, "who?" With whom does God want you to learn, share, grow, and apply His truths? Think of your friends, family, co-workers, neighbors, schoolmates, and anyone else God brings to mind. Also, consider who you would enjoy spending time with for a few weeks. Write the names down as God brings them to mind.

Begin calling today! Once you have a name or two in mind, call them today, and see if they would be willing to share their thoughts and ideas with you for a few weeks.

Once one person says yes, you may be tempted to limit it to just the two of you. However, by inviting a few others, you have created a meeting you all look forward to each week. Most people you ask have one or two other friends who would love to join, too.

Remember, you don't need 20, 10, or even 5 people for a sufficient group. The Bible says, "Where two or more have gathered, he is in their midst." The important thing is that you start with at least one other person so you can "do life together."

Check out curriculum. For many people, a study book may give them all they need to interact, but others might benefit from a DVD or video teaching series; these keep discussion flowing.

BUILDINGLIFE**TOGETHER**

Once you choose the curriculum, you may want to host an open house for your members and preview the series you choose. At this point, they can also pick up and take home the curriculum.

God desires each of us to live a good life, but He never intended us to live it alone. He modeled this with the 12 disciples. It's fascinating that many of my Christian friends (and even church leaders) ride alone like the Lone Ranger, missing out on the joy of deeper and more significant relationships with the body of Christ.

I'm ashamed to admit I have done this as well during different seasons of my life. Even after serving as the Small Group Champion at both Willow Creek and Saddleback Church, it took my wife and me several years before we created a new circle of friends. Now, I would do anything for them as they would for me.

"Doing my life" with others has taught me some of life's greatest lessons—especially that winning in life is best experienced not alone, but together.

A 30 DAY READING PLAN
FOR SMALL GROUP MINISTRY DIRECTORS

Henry Nouwen speaks to spiritual leaders and challenges them to consider a path to ministry that first starts in solitude with God. He says that effective and lasting ministry for God comes from a quiet place alone with God. This is why this 30-day journey is so important.

The "Great Adventure" of all our lives is simply found in the daily pursuit of knowing, growing, serving, sharing, and worshiping Christ forever. This is the essence of a purposeful life, to see all five biblical purposes fully formed and balanced in our lives. It's in the balance that we achieve health which ultimately leads us to the spiritual growth we all long for as believers. It's the simple focus on Paul's words to the early church when he said "to present every man and woman complete in Christ" we need to be clear about seeing all five Biblical purposes fully formed in our lives.

You and I both know this doesn't just happen. It takes a clear sense of purpose, planning, and encouragement from others. This journal is designed to give you and your group a tool to help in the process of forming Christ deep within your heart and the hearts of your people.

David poured his heart out to God in writing what we know today as the book of Psalms. That book contains his honest conversations with God in written form. They included every imaginable emotion, and integration of Old Testament scriptures and simple reflections on every aspect of his life.

I want to encourage you to carve out a few minutes to pray and plan the first steps in this journal. You can begin by reading the first story, reflection and leadership lesson, and then write down your thoughts, questions, or heart felt response to God. Don't be afraid to connect with Him and listen for those things He will place on your heart. He is your maker, and knows your every thought!

This Reading Plan is designed to apply the basic habits of reading God's word and responding to it, to create a more intimate walk with Christ. A few simple suggestions as you begin . . . as David did, select a source or strategy to integrate God's Word into your devotional time. Some helpful resources are: The Bible, The One Year Bible, New Testament Bible Challenge Reading Plan, Devotional Book, and Topical Bible Study plan.

Enjoy . . .

SESSION 1
HOW TO LAUNCH AND LEAD A SMALL GROUP MINISTRY IN YOUR CHURCH

Introduction to the Building Lifetogether Series

Church Testimonies

1. Pastor Bill has about 170 people in his church and he just got over 32 different leaders that are going to host a group in his church.

2. Charlie Holt, who had almost 300 people in his church, and he had 800 people get connected in a group. He didn't retain them all, but he retained well over 150 percent of his original 300.

How to launch and lead a small group ministry in your church

"Building a healthy balanced small group ministry will happen over time not over night"

1. _____ your entire congregation and community
   a. "No eye has seen, no ear has heard, no mind has conceived what God has prepared for those who love him"

   b. You can connect all of your congregation under the care of a shepherd.

   c. One church had about 30 percent of his congregation connected in groups and it took about six years to get that far. After working with us for about six months, he now has 30 percent of his congregation that are leaders, and 130 percent that are connected.

2. _____ an unlimited number of leaders
   a. Use the Crowd to Core strategy
      ☐ Challenge everyone to shepherd someone.
      ☐ Give them plug and play curriculum

☐ Encourage them to invite a few friends

   b. We will help you convert everyone of your members into leaders over time

3. _____ **healthy, balanced groups**
   a. Most groups are about fellowship or teaching the Bible
   b. We will help you balance the purposes in your group

4. _____ **and training your leaders for life**
   a. Move from one leader to 50-80% of every one of your members on a serving team.
   b. Everyone is called to be able to shepherd another or shepherd a few.
   c. New plug and play DVD based leader training is available to train leader of leaders.
   d. New coaching strategies where a coach pairs up with one person.
   e. New live coaching program for church leaders to receive just in time coaching.

5. _____ **a culture that celebrates your life together**
   a. Small group ministry really is not just another program. It is one of the key biblical directives that God set up in the very first place. He modeled it and designed it into the New Testament church.
   b. Worship happens in Temple Courts and house to house in the form of fellowship, breaking of bread, and prayer.

The moment you stop learning is the moment you stop leading.

Next steps from this session
Step 1. Write a few reflections on the teaching of this session

- *Seek God's heart for the dream. (Seek God's dream for our church.)*
- *Share the dream w/ others to grow w/ in this dream.*
- *Select a team to commit 6 wks to.*

Step 2. Begin praying for God's dream for your church, then share the dream with a few others.
Step 3. Select a team and raise up one person from that team to be your champion.

WHY SMALL GROUPS ARE A BIG DEAL
SEVEN THINGS EVERY PASTOR NEEDS TO KNOW ABOUT THE EMERGENCE OF SMALL GROUP MINISTRY.

There is no simple solution to growing a healthy, balanced body of believers. However, a thriving small group ministry may be one of the best ways to fulfill the biblical purposes of the church—and solve many of the issues of evangelism and stewardship that can confound pastors. Here are seven reasons why every pastor should consider investing resources into building a healthy small group ministry:

1. Small group community is a primary felt need in America, let alone in our churches.
In South Orange County, there is a community known as one of the top 10 fastest growing developments in the country. For every new home construction, there are 10,000 applications from interested buyers.

Part of the appeal of this community is that it is built from the ground up for community. Its ads sell a return to "Mayberry" days, when everyone had a front porch, a true neighborhood community, and a sense of family among friends. Their slogan is simply this: Belong.

I met the Community Director for one of these kinds of neighborhoods and was fascinated to learn that her job is to create and cultivate a sense of community—where people feel loved, supported, needed, and have a true sense of belonging. She hires, trains, and manages cul-de-sac leaders, helping them launch social events, such as progressive dinners, costume parties, and charades nights. Her job includes a weekly trip to new and existing cul-de-sacs with a truck filled with fresh Starbucks and Krispy Kreme Donuts.

This model is very simple, effective, and transferable to any church. It can work for small groups or the entire church, and is easy to establish. Encourage your members to host a back-to-school picnic, end of the summer party, or a weekend barbeque—not for the purpose of selling homes, but to see their homes used for Christ.

For example, I did this last summer by renting a bounce house on our block. It cost me $75.00 for the day, and almost every family joined in the fun. I asked every adult who came if they would be open to participating in a 6-week Bible study on the topic of marriage, family, or relationships. It was a success.

This fall, instead of trying to get the community to come to your church, why not consider bringing your church to the community?

2. Significant life transformation can happen in small groups.
Most pastors and church leaders assume small groups are a great way to create a sense of community among the members of their congregation. It's true. Small groups are a great tool for helping people transition from doing life alone to doing life together.

Rick Warren, developer of the *40 Days of Purpose* program, says small groups provide a place for people to fulfill all five purposes of the church: 1) grow warmer through fellowship, 2) deeper through discipleship, 3) stronger through worship, 4) broader through ministry, 5) and larger through evangelism.

Other Christian leaders endorse small groups, as well. Bill Hybels says "life change happens best in small groups." Rob Lacey says it's a great place for people to "talk back" about the Bible and discuss the implications of its message, leading to greater application of truth in the lives of those who attend. Bob Buford, founder of the Leadership Network, said to me recently, "There is a definite shift in the church from just a procrastination model seen in churches all across America, to a greater demonstration model of Christianity that leads to greater transformation of our hearts."

With the introduction of new DVD and video teaching delivered directly into living rooms and classrooms in our churches, we can get the best of both worlds—proclamation and devotion. The churches we have had the privilege of coaching have had a positive response about our teaching and training materials from members who say they are glad not only to have more teaching, but more talking about teaching, as well. Talking about teaching leads to greater integration of truth in the lives of people—resulting in the transformation of the minds, hearts, and hands of believers for Christ!

3. Small groups can exponentially grow your church.

Deep down, most pastors would love to grow their church. Rick Warren says, "Balancing the purpose in your church leads to growth and balance to health and that health ultimately leads to growth." But how?

As your church grows larger in attendance, you need to counteract that by simultaneously growing it "smaller" through small groups ministry. I've had the privilege of serving at two megachurches with thousands in attendance, but I grew up in a small church of less than 100 members. I now know that if my pastor would have followed some of the simple steps we learned in the "40 Days of Purpose" campaign, he could have easily doubled or tripled the active attendance in our church. 70 percent of the churches we coach and consult have healthy, active Sunday school programs, but with the addition of small group ministries they can multiply growth exponentially.

In the early 1950s, Sunday school was designed as a tool for evangelism and assimilation, but over the years, its primary purpose has been education. Today, few churches have an extra Sunday school classroom available, and the average Sunday school class size is 12 people. It's difficult to grow your church through Sunday school because brick and mortar limit growth, unless you keep building more educational space—which most churches can't afford. Don't miss the opportunity for growth through small groups community.

The beauty of off-campus groups is the potential for unlimited growth. An onsite Sunday school program is limited unless complemented with off-campus small groups. As Rick Warren says, "Don't let the shoe tell the foot how big it can grow."

Ironically, during the first 300 years of the church, people didn't meet in temple courts; they met in homes. Since then, we've done just the opposite—moved from homes to church buildings. The truth is, we need more house-to-house ministry to grow our churches.

4. Small groups are not a program, but a primary model for doing church.
I've talked with many senior pastors who say small group ministry is one of many programs in the church. But small group ministry is the primary model found in the New Testament.

The book of Acts teaches that the early church met as a church *gathered* and a church *scattered*. Somehow, we have forgotten the "scattered" church, and small group ministry can help us model the early church.

We must work together on what it takes to help our people do life together just like Jesus. And the best part about this is that Jesus didn't just tell us to do it—he modeled it through his own life and ministry. How about your church? Are your members doing life in community with a few like Jesus did? Maybe it's time.

Doing life together is a biblical model, not a fancy program.

5. Small groups ministry will become the primary means to lifestyle evangelism in the future.
Building relationships is the most non-threatening, natural way to connect authentically with an unchurched person. And your home is the best place on earth to hear the most important message in eternity. 50 percent of people invited by a friend will say yes to a short six-week Bible study in your home. 50 percent!

If you simply challenge your people to follow God's call to do life together, it will have a positive impact on your church. Ask church members to write down names of 6-10 people with whom they would enjoy doing life together and challenge them to call those people on that list this week. Then, create a video table they can check out after each Sunday service. Provide DVD/Video curriculum with a few study guides for the week so they can have the tools they need to be able to host Bible studies in their homes with their friends. Challenge them with the value of community.

Here is the best part! We've found that in at least 40 percent of the churches we work with, when people jot down the names of friends to invite to their group, most don't worry if those friends are Christian or not. They just ask, "Is this someone I'd like to do life together with or hang out with for six weeks?" So they end up inviting people who do not know Christ, are new in their relationship with Christ, are not growing in their relationship with Christ, have never been in a small group, or haven't made spiritual life decisions in a long time.

6. Small groups are the crock-pot for training unlimited leaders.
Bill Hybels said at the Leadership Summit last August, that small groups were one of the top performance drivers in the church of tomorrow. Rick Warren said they are a "Leadership Engine or Factory of the Future." Either way, don't underestimate the power of community to train and develop the leaders of the future.

I call it the crock-pot method, because mobilizing small-group leaders is getting easy. The real challenge is developing leaders who don't just launch a group for six weeks, but leaders who continue on for a lifetime. Here are a few ideas that can work right away for you.

First, challenge all groups to de-emphasize apprenticeship and focus on rotating and sharing leadership. The best way to learn how to lead is to experience it. This will grow every member into a leader … not overnight but over time. When you rotate leadership in the groups, ultimately people are being better prepared than if they were to participate in a 10-week small group leadership training course. Each person gets a turn to lead and passes the curriculum on to the next person to facilitate the next time.

Second, use campaigns two or three times a year to align the weekend with the small group study to create an excuse to ask all existing groups to take a six-week vacation to host a short-term group in their community for their church community. 30 percent of the Saddleback groups did this during our first 40 Day Campaign. But you could do this every fall, even if you have done it before in the past. The Beginning Lifetogether DVD is an excellent resource for our first small group campaign. You could launch 20-40 percent of your church into groups. It comes with live weekly teaching (from Bruce Wilkenson, John Ortberg, Henry Cloud, Joe Stowell, etc.), live leader training, live testimonial, and live small group worship. It's the first plug-and-play curriculum on the market with a built-in small group leader "GPS" system for your leaders. Do it again every fall, even if you have done 40 Days before. Each week, a new teacher shares about one of the five purposes, helping bring back the vision and momentum gained from the previous campaign. It will amaze you as it did us at Saddleback!

Third, give them plug-and-play DVD/video curriculum. Not everyone is called to be a teacher or a leader, but some are called to be shepherds of a few.

7. Small groups will help to increase weekly giving and the response to any capital campaign.
Glen Kruen, the executive pastor at Saddleback, said that giving increased well over 25 percent during the "40 Days of Purpose" campaign. This was true across the country. Not only will a church's weekly giving rise, but when they have a capital campaign, they will see a significant return on their investment.

I have seen this work with every church we have coached. Many of these churches postponed their campaigns until after they connected another 25-75 percent of their church into groups. This is critical not only because it will improve the overall financial health of the church, but the spiritual health, as well—and it is the spiritual benefits that are vital to factor in when considering church finances.

Willow Creek's executive pastor Greg Hawkins, who ran its capital campaign, said that over 60 percent of the people who gave to the capital campaign to raise over $75 million for their new facility came from people in small groups. Overall, the water level in any church's giving goes up. When people are cared for and feel loved, there's a tendency for them to give more. One pastor likened it to when Peter was fishing all day on one side of the boat and then Jesus instructed him to toss his nets on the other side.

Well, how about you? If you consider all these ideas that have worked in other churches, I promise that you won't come home empty. Instead, the people in your community will be more likely to come home where they belong!

SMALL GROUP SUCCESS ISN'T JUST FOR MEGA CHURCHES!

I can remember it like it was yesterday. I had been on staff at Saddleback Church for only a few weeks when I learned that more than 800 men from our congregation were planning to attend the Promise Keepers rally in Washington, D.C. I suggested we try to launch some new small groups among the men going to the event. More than 300 said they were interested, but I only had half a dozen men to lead them -- the story of a small group pastor's life.

I got to game day, where everybody showed up to get into a group, and I tried something called the "small group connection" process. People gather into pairs, then fours, and then groups of eight according to where they live. The process simply allows people to traverse down a spiral of questions. The group moves from icebreaker-like questions into deeper spiritual conversation. This allows them to discern the spiritual shepherd (not leader) in the circle. This model follows the Acts 6 example, where the disciples encouraged the people to select from among the church seven people to serve tables.

We launched 32 groups that day with almost 300 people. We saw some disasters, but we also had a seed of an idea that helped to serve the church-wide small group campaigns for years to come. No longer did we have a problem finding leaders. We were providing the living rooms of every ministry with pre-qualified leaders.

We refined the process with training, coaching, and raising up co-leaders. The big addition was what we called the "Rick Factor." The secret weapon in any church for recruiting new leaders is and always will be the senior pastor. In one weekend, we signed up more than 1,500 people wanting to get into a group.

So we had the number one recruiter on our side, but we still had only 50 percent of average weekend attendance connected in a group. Progress had been made, but we still had 8,000 to 12,000 people to go before we felt we were fulfilling what God had called us to do.

The solution came to us on the eve of the 40 Days of Purpose campaign at Saddleback: videotape of Rick teaching the material. Finally, ordinary members could be leaders because they didn't need the same skills for teaching, facilitation, and knowledge of the Scripture as Rick had. With the new video curriculum we were able to simply say, "If you have a VCR, you can be a star."

Anybody can host a group like this! And they did. Our team trained more than 2,000 new hosts and launched another 2,300 groups with more than 20,000 people going through a six-week study on The Purpose Driven Life. It truly was "exceedingly abundantly beyond what we asked

BUILDING LIFETOGETHER

or thought," as Paul says.

Was that just because it was Saddleback? I thought so, until I had the opportunity to talk with literally thousands of other churches using our new Doing Lifetogether™ curriculum. Over the last few years, I've seen with my own eyes that any church of any size could do the same thing we have done.

The bottom line is that you have to ask a very basic question: "What is the point of 40 Days of Purpose -- or any spiritual or small group campaign for that matter?" It should be to help the people in the church live healthy, balanced Purpose Driven lives. It's not about connecting people into community for the sake of community, but about changing community through community in order to convert our culture for the sake of Christ.

That's what Jesus came to do, after all -- not just in the upper room but also at the cross, so that we might do our lives together with him and one another.

IMAGINE CONNECTING 25% TO 50% OF YOUR CONGREGATION!

Rick Warren taught The Purpose Driven Life to almost 40,000 people at Saddleback Easter services this last weekend. I was one of the many that sat glued to the video monitor with couples and one single mom that got connected in a small group at Saddleback just this last year.

Where would they be had pastor Rick not challenged 2,600 people to open up their home and host a six-week study on The Purpose Driven Life? Why not challenge your congregation these next two weeks to consider stepping out in faith and giving the gift of Easter away to a few friends?

There are two ways to look at your Easter crowd. One way is to look down on the Easter lily crowd and to mentally ridicule their lack of faithfulness. The other way is to see how people are spiritually drawn to your church at Easter like no other time of the year. Granted, some folks are there to wear their new outfit, then go out to brunch. But, many are seeking a connection with the risen Christ. And the two weeks following Easter this year could be one of the greatest opportunities to connect them into a group.

This Easter is unique because the early date will allow you to start groups for a study they could finish before summer begins. Here are some keys to making this time a spring of another kind.

1. Clarify the vision. What are you trusting God for this Easter? What does God want to accomplish that you may have no idea how to pull off? What if you could connect another 25-50% of your average adult attendance in small groups? What does God want to do this spring? In Matthew 9:36, we see how Jesus had compassion on the multitudes who were harassed and helpless, like a sheep without a shepherd. Our challenge is to develop a shepherd for every sheep. But, this vision is much larger than merely connecting the Body together. Christ's vision is to reach the world and make disciples. What better place to gather a group of believers or non-believers together to study God's Word than in the home of church members in order to fulfill the Great Commission?

The vision needs to first start with you and then be cast to your congregation. God's heart is for your members and Easter attenders to not do their life alone but, to do their life together. The question is less a matter of "if" but more about "when" and with "whom" to do it

2. Connect your series with a service. If you've done a 40 Days campaign with Purpose Driven, then you understand the dynamic that is created with everyone in a small group doing a study that goes along with the Sunday morning message. There's a great sense of unity. You can easily create this dynamic in your church by selecting a small group study from the Experiencing Christ Together curriculum, then creating a message series that focuses on each theme of the study.

By aligning your weekend message with a small group study, you can easily launch a large number of groups two Sundays after Easter. This is an excellent series after Easter. First, because people are reminded of the work Jesus did on the cross, and second, every Christ-follower and even seeker wants to know him better.

Sometimes you want to not just link the sermon and a study but even your worship in the "big house" with worship in the "small house" (including Sunday school). The Lifetogether Worship series is a breakthrough small group worship experience delivered right into the living room or classroom. This new resource could be used and encouraged in the weekend music during worship and expanded in the homes during the week. This new series, collaborated with Maranatha! Music, provides a great way to enlarge the heart of worship in your church.

3. Catalyze unlimited leaders. Believe it or not, there are mature, knowledgeable followers of Christ sitting in your church that are more than able to facilitate a Bible discussion with a DVD-based curriculum. I talked with a church recently that recruited 300 new hosts in one weekend. Charlie Robinson, a pastor in a small church of 300, recruited 52 new hosts to lead a six week Doing Life Together Series last Easter, and 37 of those groups are still growing and going strong. Don't underestimate what God can do. Read the article "A 'Blockbuster' Small Group Strategy" (in Case Studies section in Appendix).

The only reason individuals are not leading groups is that they've never been asked. We have seen many senior pastors invite their members to get into the game from the pulpit right in the middle of their Sunday morning message. All you need to do is let your people know that if they will open up their hearts and their homes to a circle of friends, that you will support them in starting a group. This invitation could be just as simple as putting a card in your bulletin and asking folks to fill it out and place it in the offering plate. Follow this up with a brief orientation to get them started.

Now, if you have groups that have been in the game for a while, this is the time to challenge them to branch out. Invite your established groups to take a six-week vacation from their current group to lead a new group.

Jesus went to the cross on Easter for them; are they willing to create a community for him? All you ask for is six weeks -- no more or less. At the end of those six weeks, they are more than welcome to return to their groups. At Saddleback, we saw 30 percent of our groups (leaders and members) volunteer for a six-week vacation. The net effect of that exponentially multiplied the number of hosts that could lead a group for just a few weeks.

Jesus instructed us to pray to the Lord of the harvest to send forth laborers (Matthew 9:38). The harvest is plentiful. The workers are few. But, the workers are there. If you invite your members to try a six-week study, you will be amazed at the number of people who will step up to do this. You will be more amazed at the number who will continue. I have seen first hand the number of churches in our coaching programs get well over 30 percent of their average adult attendance hosting a group. This is no longer an anomaly but a dream come true straight from the heart of Christ the Shepherd.

4. Challenge everyone to participate. The key is that the more folks you get into the game on the host/leader side virtually guarantees a larger harvest on the participant side. As the senior pastor leads the way by not only promoting groups but in leading a group, others will catch the vision for groups.

Every new host has a circle of friends, neighbors, co-workers, and family. If each new host would put two or three names in each of those categories, then you have more than enough for a group. But a group doesn't have to be 12. A group could be two or three with Christ in their midst.

Easter Sunday is over, but the next two Sundays are critical. There isn't much time to put this in place, but you can do some key things to maximize the impact of Easter. Something as simple as selecting an easy to use, DVD-based curriculum and putting a sign up form in the bulletin, can take your church to places of connection in groups that you have never seen before. If you don't feel like you can pull off a full-blown launch this week, then run a pilot -- in a Sunday school class, from one service, a few small groups, or just trust us on this one, and play a 90 second preview (on every Lifetogether series) and see what God does.

5. Create healthy, balanced groups. The curriculum your group uses is really the key. Both the Doing Life Together series and the Experiencing Christ Together series or any Saddleback curriculum series, balance the five biblical purposes in each lesson. The curriculum provides the balance for groups to connect with each other, dig into God's Word, act on God's Word, focus on outreach, and surrender to God. The curriculum is structured so that each person in the group can facilitate the discussion. This puts everyone in the role to need to trust God before the lesson. Sweaty palms are a great incentive to get into God's Word and to seek God's face before each meeting.

6. Coach and train your leaders for life. Training your new and even your existing leaders can be difficult. I have sat many times in near empty rooms praying for more than a few leaders to attend. One rainy night even at Saddleback I had two leaders show up. I went home early discouraged and committed to do something about it. The new DVD small group leader training series Hosting Lifetogether is just the solution. It's flexible in delivery, transferable for anybody, and honestly, sold at almost my cost. I just don't want leaders to go untrained and small group champions to struggle like I did. We recommend ordering one journal and DVD for each leader.

Many pastors are tempted to lecture their potential leaders for weeks on end before they release them for leadership. The problem is that after weeks and weeks of training, you still really don't know that person or what they might do in their group. The best way to know what's happening in a group is to get to know the leader really well. Now, if your group launch is successful, then you will immediately have more groups than the typical senior pastor or small group champion can touch base with.

What we've found is that if you start your new hosts off in the right direction with an orientation and introduce each host to an experienced leader who will walk alongside them for six weeks, you can easily deliver the training that each host needs when they need it and personally get to know each host.

This simple concept is a breakthrough in the traditional coaching model that honestly doesn't work very well. No other strategy works better at getting to know hosts this well in such a short period of time. Call them "buddies" or "small group mentors" for simply helping a "new host" or leader survive the first six weeks.

Your existing leaders are the key to building the support structure that your new hosts will need. By simply calling the new host each week after their meeting, answering their questions, encouraging them and praying for them, new hosts will have the support to keep going and to keep on the right track. Coaching Lifetogether is an excellent tool to help first time coaches to build into the lives of brand new hosts and further develop existing leaders.

7. Create connecting campaigns multiple times. What's better than doing one large campaign per year is to launch groups in sequential campaigns throughout the year. We've found that the best times of year to launch groups are fall, New Year's and spring. Each campaign builds on the next. Something as simple as announcing a fall series in late April or early May will sustain your groups over the summer. Some groups might want to get together for social times and service opportunities during the summer. Other groups might get out their calendars and find six dates where they can fit in a summertime series. Either way, groups that like each other just need an excuse to continue.

What is God's vision for your Easter? Why not try something new? You may feel like you are risking it all -- maybe your life. That's nothing less than what Jesus did. I'd suggest you give it a try. You can make it a spring of another kind -- it might just change your life and bring new life to your congregation.

BUILDINGLIFETOGETHER

FROM DREAM TO REALITY

MOST LEADERS WHO DREAM OF "FINDING A SHEPHERD FOR EVERY SHEEP" FIND THEMSELVES A BIT LOST WHEN IT COMES TO STARTING SMALL GROUPS. YOU'RE NOT ALONE.

At Lifetogether, we say,"Fall is to small group ministry, what Easter is to the church"—that is, if you want to launch a small group ministry, do it in the fall. You can also, of course, start one in January or after Easter, but there's nothing like the fall to give you momentum for the entire school year.

Here are 5 steps to help you turn your dream of starting a small group ministry into a reality.

1. Pray for God to help you gather a few folks to help you. Okay, so that isn't a profound insight. But you can't do it alone. How many do you need? A handful or two … but they need to have the heart for small group ministry—as well as the gift of leadership. They also need a passion for reaching your neighborhood and community for Christ. One more thing: do this with people you like. Make sure you would enjoy having them on your team. This process should be both fruitful and fun.

2. Meet with the Senior Pastor or Staff Leadership. You may need to cast the vision for "transforming lives through community." Ask your pastor or church staff if they would come to your first meeting and listen to a few tapes and review the some ideas about your curriculum. More importantly, ask them to share their dreams about community not only with their congregation but their community for Christ. Just watch their vision rise and ownership increase. If you are the staff leadership, do the same with your volunteer team.

3. Develop a simple plan. You need a basic understanding of what you're trying to accomplish and how that fits with your church's overall vision. Be sure to have your entire leadership team watch the *Building Lifetogether* videos at the same time as a discussion starter.

4. Launch your groups in one of the three key windows. That is, as mentioned above, in September, in January, or in April-after-Easter. As I mentioned earlier, the best time is definitely during the fall season. It's the "Easter" of small group ministry. People expect something new in the fall.

5. Select your small group kick-off curriculum series. It's critical that you have a curriculum for the entire year. There is so much great material being published for small groups. The big issue is how to choose something that fits your strategy moving forward. With our Lifetogether product line, we recommend the first book in the 36 week "Doing Lifetogether" curriculum, called "Beginning" or the second "Connecting with Your Church Family"—which includes not only the study but the corresponding teaching DVD.

In starting a small group, it's vital to remember that it's most important that you start. Do something. Get going. You may find initially that you have some big wins and some big losses building your your small group community. Ultimately, if your groups are kept healthy, the wins will out-weigh the losses, and the ministry will flourish over time.

12 STEPS IN PLANNING YOUR SMALL GROUP LAUNCH

Step 1: Create a One Year of Ministry Plan and ask your Senior Pastor to align sermons two times during the year, once either before or after Easter and the second in the fall. Use the One Year of Ministry Planner as your guide to plan the themes and order of material for the small groups. Tie the themes to the overall vision of the church. One church had the year of the leader last year and this year the year of discipleship. At minimum leverage the themes of the purposes in the sermon series during the launch periods. If you start groups by mid-January do Connect and Share before Easter then Grow and Shape after Easter. You could also do a launch with either Connect or Grow before Easter and Grow or Connect after Easter.

Step 2: Get the Senior Pastor on board early. The Senior Pastor is the key small group champion and host recruiter. It gives so much credibility to your efforts when your Senior Pastor says he's hosting a group and he is behind the launch.

Ask him to:
a) Promote from the pulpit do the ask for hosting in the middle of the sermons.
b) Model the way by hosting a group.
c) Ask current groups to take a 6 week vacation.
d) Help recruit community leaders and follow up with a thank you to them.
e) Sponsor a leadership core vision casting rally 3-4 weeks before launch.
f) Commission the new hosts during the worship service.
g) Align sermons with curriculum during the 6 week initial launch.
h) Celebrate the groups and God at the end of the 6 weeks.

Step 3: Prepare for Promotion. Recruit and record testimonies and sound bites. Use the Coaching resource DVD with testimonies or create your own. John Maxwell, Gary Smalley, Joel Osteen, Rhonda Schroder, Gary Kendall and others give great testimonies of small groups. Write promotion themes prior to each launch and pick appropriate stories and testimonies to be shared. Always look for the reluctant person that had a great experience. Use skits or reluctant leader and member stories to share the vision and value of changed lives. Select weekends that you will promote it from the pulpit and get it on the Worship service schedule as early as you can.

Step 4: Share your One Year of Ministry Plan. Share it with the church staff and small groups

then during each season ask the Senior Pastor to share the purpose theme and talk about what the small groups are doing from the pulpit. Give him the book or a flier to hold up during the service. Ask the Senior Pastor to tie it to a sermon topic about community. Feed him testimonies and stories early enough to give him time to weave things into his sermons. Ask the Senior Pastor to send out an email with the vision and plan for the next launch. Include testimonies of reluctant hosts and prayer request for the larger community.

Step 5. Recruit & Train Community Leaders and Coaches. Build your sustainable small groups by investing in a leadership team to help you. Whether it's 1 person or 100 people, it will be the best investment you can make to sustain community in your congregation. Meet with them weekly for a while as you begin. Invest in them. The *Coaching Lifetogether* DVD series is perfect to train them. It will be your greatest return on investment.

Step 6: Invest in your current hosts. Share the inside story with them before you go public. Host a half-day retreat or vision casting session for the community leaders and small group team to mobilize and motivate them. Use the Hosting Lifetogether DVD for less experienced leaders and Coaching Life

Step 7: Call for hosts multiple weeks in a row from the pulpit. Include 1-2 sermons on community 2-4 weeks before the launch. During one use the circles of life and ask everyone in the congregation to fill one out. Then use the ABC strategy (Ask God, Begin calling, Check out material).

Step 8: Pray as a staff and a small group community for those on the circles of life. Find a way to get a copy of the forms and hold a day of prayer specifically for the hosts and those they will invite. Encourage everyone in the church to join you as you pray. Send out prayer updates and testimonies of answered prayer. Include personal prayer requests from the Senior Pastor and staff. Encourage the small group to do prayer walks in their neighborhood and pray for the people in their neighborhood.

Step 9: Do a host briefing with the Senior Pastor on the weekend. Make it practical and visionary. Provide a host packet of material and focus on connected the hosts with a Community Leader or coach and helping them fill their groups. Show the Hosts how to access the just in time training on the DVD and the training resources in the back of the study guide. Then, toward the end of the campaign before the next series ask the community leaders to help gather Hosts in their homes to view the leading life together material together and discuss it.

Step 10. Do a Host rally 2-3 weeks prior to the launch. Use it as a catalytic event to share the vision for the year with the core of the church. Show how the small group launch is tied to the vision of the church. Use testimonies and the Circles of Life exercise to cast vision of reaching the community through small groups.

Step 11. Align the sermons with the small group material.

Step 12. Plan a celebration for the end of the 6 weeks.

SESSION 2
CONNECT YOUR ENTIRE CONGREGATION INTO COMMUNITY

Purpose of Fellowship

What is the model, motivation and method for connection your entire congregation?

1. _____
   - ☐ Early church – Acts 2:42
   - ☐ Temple Courts & House to House
   - ☐ One another's in New Testament
   - ☐ Cast vision to connect, grow, and serve, just what Jesus told us to do

2. _____:
   - ☐ every stage of life including children
   - ☐ any size of church
   - ☐ any theological belief
   - ☐ any denominational background
   - ☐ any geographical region
   - ☐ any church tradition

3. _____
   - ☐ Sociological needs
   - ☐ Viral / organic
   - ☐ Form to function
   - ☐ Who are you doing life with

4. _____
   - ☐ Greatest Spiritual Formation Engines
   - ☐ Financial stewardship of the church
   - ☐ Core Initiatives
   - ☐ Care for people (heart)
   - ☐ Class system for increasing membership

5. _____
   - ☐ Exponential
   - ☐ Connects congregation
   - ☐ Larger & Smaller at the same time
   - ☐ Every member missionary
   - ☐ Every Sheep has a Shepherd

6. _____
   - ☐ Seeker
   - ☐ Student
   - ☐ Servant
   - ☐ Shepherd
   - ☐ Supervisor
   - ☐ Staff

7. _____
   - ☐ DVD and video based teaching curriculum
   - ☐ Ordinary people with an extraordinary experience
   - ☐ Like a Gutenberg Press, it introduces multiplying transferable resources
   - ☐ Empower people to create their own community

8. _____
   - ☐ A leader will assimilate 10 members
   - ☐ Promotional tools you can use on the weekend
   - ☐ Brochures for members to pre-order the curriculum for a year
   - ☐ Everybody's got a home
   - ☐ Everybody's got friends
   - ☐ Encourage them to H.O.S.T. a group
   - ☐ Circles of Life
   - ☐ Who you going to call….

9. _____
   - ☐ Church Leaders
   - ☐ Core
   - ☐ Committed
   - ☐ Crowd

10. _____
    - ☐ Natural flow for assimilation
      a. Fall
      b. Winter
      c. Spring
    - ☐ Next step series - Needed Curriculum (5 purposes, fellowship or surrender)

Next steps from this session
Step 1. Write a few reflections on the teaching of this session

_____

_____

_____

1. Create a One Year Plan.
2. Select your Assimilation Curriculum

RECONNECTING THE CONNECTED
HOW ONE CHURCH BUILT GROUPS FROM NATURAL AFFINITY GROUPS.

When our church took a health assessment, we made an interesting discovery: People who were not in small groups rated themselves just as highly in fellowship/connectedness as people who were in small groups.

We used to view our church as hundreds of disconnected souls in desperate need of community. But we learned everyone in our church is connected to someone: a family member, co-workers, customers, neighbors, and friends.

We wondered, How do we convince people who think they're connected that they really aren't, and get them into small groups?

The solution was simple. Our Senior Pastor invited anyone who would like to do a study with their friends to take the materials after the service. The curriculum went like hot cakes. In fact, after our second service, I had to tell our Senior Pastor to quit asking, because we ran out of material.

Rick, one of our most passionate leaders, told us that leading this group is the best thing he's ever done. However, he never would have done it without a nudge.

There were many other Ricks out there, reluctant to lead a small group. Think about the demands of a small group. First, we ask them to do a 6-week Bible study, probably for the first time. Then, we ask them to take an extra hour out of their week. Finally, we ask them to spend this extra hour doing the study with a group of strangers. Sounds like a recipe for failure, doesn't it?

By inviting our members to do a 6-week study with people they were already connected to, we gave them an excuse to get together with people they already knew and loved. Not only did these groups form faster, but they are lasting longer.

Three women who already met every Thursday for coffee at Starbucks are now doing a Bible study together. Bored commuters on a train from Central California to the Bay Area are spending wasted time studying God's Word together. Employees in the break room of an overhead door company spend their lunchtime doing the small group study.

Once the unconnected were connected, we worried about how to get to know everyone. We learned you couldn't; however, you can get to know each host. Each of our new hosts receives support from a small group coach, their "buddy," who has some experience—at least one 6-week study's worth. They call the new host each week after their meeting to see how it went, pray for them, and answer any questions they might have.

In the fall, 40 percent of our new small groups started by inviting our church members to pick up the curriculum and get together with their friends. Today, 100 percent of our new groups have started this way.

What's our biggest problem now? We have to convince them that they actually *are* small groups. But that's the least of our worries.

WHEN YOU REALIZE NUMBERS DON'T MATTER

Why small group success can't be measured by numbers.

Every time our church tried to launch a new small group ministry, we failed. Things never turned out the way we hoped. For our fall launch, we began planning five months in advance, which left us feeling like we had things under control. Though we earnestly worked to make it an outreach event, we launched only two groups—and those two groups were comprised of only longtime church members.

It was heart-wrenching to see our endeavor flop on its face.

When we analyzed why it didn't work, we began to examine our motives. Ultimately, we realized we were only concerned about numbers—not about lives being transformed.

We learned that when you launch small groups as a willing sacrifice with the purest of motives, you don't need results to be successful. You just need to know that you did what you were supposed to do.

While you want to be hopeful and positive about results, you have to be realistic and know you might not get the results you expect. This is true sacrifice: giving up your expectations and accepting God's will.

True sacrifice also entails being willing to get out of the boat to let somebody else in the boat. It's risky; you could die in the process, but you're willing because you know if you don't, others won't be rescued.

So you enter into that Hebrews 11 Hall of Fame group that had a promise but never saw the results. That's biblical. I do believe we're going to be rewarded—that someday there will be numbers. But we haven't seen them yet.

If I were living just for large numbers, I don't think I would have continued, because results aren't always immediate.

Our lay people have worked really hard and long on promoting and overseeing the development of small groups. We all thought our ministry was going to explode, but it never happened. That may be devastating for some people. But when your ultimate desire isn't to have thousands of people in small groups—but just to have small groups that are transforming lives—it's not.

LAUNCHING COMMUNITY
THREE STEPS TO MAKING YOUR SMALL GROUP DREAM COME TRUE FOR YOUR CHURCH

So many of us have been there—you wake up in the middle of the night feeling pulled toward starting a small group ministry at your church. But by morning you still have no clue how to go about it.

I'll tell you this: If you're a pastor wondering how to go about launching a small group ministry, start by asking yourself, "Is a small group ministry something I truly value and can excite others with?" This is crucial because values manifest themselves not in your belief system but in your behavior. If your hands and feet are not sitting somewhere where you are sharing, it will be difficult for you to have conviction about the ministry from the pulpit, in your Sunday school class or in your own small group.

Then you should ask yourself, "Do I really believe in doing life together?" Here's what I mean by this: Pastors and teachers often have trouble understanding and appreciating the value of small group ministry because they are used to telling people what to do versus talking about what they should do. Telling people what to do in community versus doing life in community is night and day. Whether or not the pastor feels the need for community doesn't change the fact that there is a need. And if you build it, they will come.

Think about this: The early church in the first 300 years did not even have temple court. It was all house to house. In modern-day American churches, we have given up on house to house and have leaned primarily on temple courts or class to class. Nowhere in the Scripture does it say "class to class." It says house to house, and that implies back in the community—not on the campus. Are you willing to take a fresh look at the biblical model in Acts and the other passages in the Bible that can't be lived out in the context of the Sunday morning message?

If you truly believe that life change and spiritual formation happen best in small settings, you can launch a small group ministry quite easily because of systems already in place. While it may seem overwhelming, there's not a lot of labor involved. Here's what you need to do:

1. Preach on it and ask people during the service if they would be willing to host a small group Bible study in their home.

2. Gather those people in your home the next week, and you have your volunteer team. You can launch a small group ministry in 30 days or less with the resources that are available. You can buy the ingredients and make a gourmet meal or you can order take out. You can make home movies or rent for the video store. A pastor does not need to create his or her own materials. Much is available.

3. Be willing to lead from weakness. Here is an example: John led a group. On the third night there, a question was asked and John couldn't answer. He couldn't answer another question, and another. Finally, he confessed that he had been busy that week and hadn't done the lesson. He was embarrassed and sorry and he couldn't fake it. He promised to do better next week. Everyone was drawn to John because he was honest. John realized the leader does not have to be perfect.

Small groups are the spiritual family system of the future. I know this, because as we see throughout Scripture, this was God's idea first.

FROM SOLOIST TO CHOIR
HOW ONE CHURCH TRANSFORMED ITS SUNDAY SCHOOL MINISTRY THROUGH SMALL GROUPS

Sunday school is one of the best places to begin building community in your church, but often Sunday school consists of star teachers—and few people end up in leadership as a result. This is the story of how one church moved from a soloist (the rock-star Sunday school teacher) mentality to a choir (a host of people providing leadership) philosophy of Sunday school ministry.

At Glen Ellyn Covenant Church in Glen Ellyn, IL, the vision and planning team decided that one of the first steps in implementing a new church vision was through the adult Sunday school program. For 12 weeks this fall, the entire adult Sunday school met in the church gym to watch the Doing Life Together DVD Teaching Series. Following the 20-minute DVD teaching clip, circled their chairs, people divided up into groups of 8 to 10, and then discussed the questions from the Doing Life Together study guides.

The vision and planning team recruited three sets of moderators (three couples), who opened the Sunday school time with prayer and announcements and Scripture reading. They recruited three sets because they knew that out of 12 weeks, one set of moderators would, likely, burn out; it's difficult for anyone to provide leadership for 12 straight weeks.

After the introduction, which included reading the Scripture passage provided by the curriculum and DVD, the moderators transitioned into the DVD teaching clip. Each lesson was visually interesting and the speakers were outstanding.

After the DVD teaching time, the moderators asked all the "fenceposts" to stand up. Twenty-five fenceposts—or discussion guides—had been recruited to lead the discussions following the teaching. So, people circled their chairs around each fencepost, who then led the group in follow-up discussions. They also recruited more fenceposts each week than were needed, because, again, they knew that few would make all 12 Sundays. They wanted to spread out the work.

What happened was amazing—instead of Sunday school starting off with 140 people and ending up with 70 or 80 at the end of the fall, attendance stayed high the entire time. Instead of one Sunday school class being led by one or two teachers, more than 30 people were involved in some kind of leadership—as a fencepost, as a moderator, or as a hospitality (food) coordinator. The 15-minute time at the beginning of Sunday school for coffee and snacks (fruit, coffee cake, etc.) proved just as valuable as the content portion!

The fall program gave the church a new vision for how Sunday school can support the larger issue of spiritual formation and life change. Their purpose was to "do life together" as a congregation this fall, and the Sunday school portion was fully integrated in accomplishing what they set out to do.

SMALL GROUPS BUILT TO LAST
HOW TO PREVENT STALE GROUPS

Often small groups become a place in the church, where "every person (or small group) does what is right in his own eyes." Too often small groups operate independently like nation states, where the individual groups choose curriculum, choose frequency of meeting, and refuse any governing or leadership structure but their own. Everything tends to move toward chaos.

If that's where your small group ministry is, then this is the time to build some health into the system. Here are a couple ideas to move your groups toward small group wellness:

1. Launch a fresh small group campaign. There's nothing like fresh wave of small groups to energize your ministry.

2. Align the launch with your weekend service. We recommend getting your pastor on board. Perhaps he could preach a six-week series on a topic, perhaps from the parables of Jesus. Use these six weeks to meet in homes as an entire church family during the series. Prepare a handout of discussion questions from the sermon as means for people to connect and grow in the six-week campaign.

3. Recruit Hosts, not leaders. The bottleneck, in building health into your small group ministry is always new leaders. Fresh troops are hard to recruit, but our strategy is not to recruit leaders; it's to recruit people who are simply willing to open their homes for a specific length of time. Instead, a couple weeks before the six-week preaching series is to begin, have your pastor make this invitation:

"In a couple weeks, we are going to 'do church together' in a way we've never done before. For six weeks, I'm going to preach through a series titled 'Growing Deeper in Our Life Together.' We would like our entire church to meet in homes each week during this time—for only six weeks. Would you open your home to a group of 8 to 10 people for six weeks? If so, then sign up at our Host Home table in Fellowship Hall after the service."

You'll be amazed how a simple change of language will open the floodgates of recruits.

Are these Hosts leaders?

Not yet. You're recruiting them to open their homes, and your team will need to coach them weekly through the six weeks as they serve coffee and get the discussion started. For resources on coaching leaders, you may want to consider our "Coaching Lifetogether" video series. The idea is recruit people on what they know they can do—open their homes and put on a pot of coffee.

4. Publicly invite your church to the host homes. Before the the six week campaign, once you recruited enough Hosts, have your pastor publicly invite your church to attend a Host Home. Then, develop a plan to have your hosts invite their 8 to 10 people with a handwritten note or letter, also calling them before the first host home meeting.

5. Roll the Host Home groups into ongoing small groups. This requires a strategy to identify leaders that emerge in the Host Homes during the six weeks. Look for additional articles to help you do this. Also make sure you have a clear curriculum plan moving forward and a way to coach your new leaders as they learn to lead.

It's often impossible to try to move existing, closed groups towards health. It's almost always best to create health by launch new groups and training your new leaders in your new ministry strategy.

SESSION 3
CULTIVATE AN UNLIMITED NUMBER OF LEADERS TO REACH YOUR COMMUNITY FOR CHRIST

Purpose of Evangelism

"Now to Him who is able to do exceedingly abundantly above all that we ask or think..."
Eph 3:20

How do you communicate to the entire congregation? — *It's a call of obedience!*

1. Remember the **CALL** of Christ on everyone of the members in your congregation
   a. "Therefore go and make disciples of all nations" Matthew 28:19
   b. Jesus asked him the third time, "Do you love me?" He said, "Lord, you know all things; you know that I love you." Jesus said, "Feed my sheep." John 21:16-18

2. **Challenge** everyone to shepherd one *(small grp vacation)*
   a. Each member can serve in another group for 6 weeks then return to your group
   b. Leave your group and start a new group
   c. You stay in one and start another

3. **Communicate** to the entire congregation
   a. Terminology matters
      1. Don't say evangelism because it scares people
      2. Be more ordinary, say watch it with a few folks that you enjoy hanging out with *(Gather a group & grow)*
   b. Cast vision on the weekend like never, ever before
   c. Do sermon alignment with a small group series
   d. You must have real live testimonies
   e. Pass out an audio or video clip on the way out of the service so they can get a broader picture
   f. Lower the bar and have more people join in. Ask everyone to open up their hearts and open up their homes and ~~HOST~~ *gather* a group. Minimize the questions in order to maximize the response.
      1. Do you have a **H**ome?
      2. Are you willing to **O**pen up your heart and home? — *Pray about it*
      3. Can you share a few **S**nacks?
      4. Will you **T**ell a few friends? *(what I did w/ grp now)*

4. **Curriculum** helps people connect.
   a. Take a little pulse of where you are then decide on the next curriculum series
   b. Announce the next series from the pulpit
   c. Show a promo piece
   d. Have them pre-order them on a bulletin insert

5. Use **Campaign** and a one year pathway, to help make this happen over time. Your goals are to launch 'em, lead 'em, and then have them continue to last over

BUILDINGLIFETOGETHER   37

the long haul.

6. Different C<u>onstiguents</u> within your congregation. Build a crowd core strategy
   a. Core: I need you to HOST a group
   b. Committed: It's time for you to create your own community. Consider your lists in life. (who's on your speed dail, Christmas cards etc.)
   c. Crowd: It's not forever, just for six weeks. Watch the series. Hang with a friend. Who do you wanna hang with? It doesn't have to be 22, it could be with just a few.

7. Message to the <u>Senior Pastor</u> (Tim Harlow)
   a. You are the number one influencer in encouraging people to be in small groups.
   b. Listen to some of the stuff Rick has done
   c. Understand the power of the pulpit
   d. Practice with a pilot
   e. Give it a try

8. Message to the <u>small group pastor (Ricki+Leslie)</u>
   a. Be patient with your pastors
   b. Prepare dual pathways, one for Sunday School and one for small groups
   — By invitation not mandatory.

9. C<u>oach</u> your existing groups
   a. turn your small groups into the most effective training incubator greenhouse
   b. Rotate the role of leadership.
   c. Ask them for a 10 percent tithe of their time
   d. Recruit Community Leaders to guide the groups   *Ask Them*

10. Tools for training and getting groups going
    a. Bring them to a briefing
    b. Use the just in time training with the DVD based lessons
    c. Hold regional DVD based training seminar
    ~~d. Use Life Together Online.~~
    ~~e. Zoomerang.com~~
    f. Constant Contact: a free newsletter system
    Short amih video.

Next steps from this session
Step 1. Write a few reflections on the teaching of this session

_____

_____

_____

Jesus looked back at the disciples, and he said, "Pray to the Lord of the harvest to send forth workers." And he didn't say worker, he said workers. And as you think about all the leaders that you have, you want to be praying for the multiple levels of leadership that you need.

FIVE STRATEGIES FOR SUSTAINING MOMENTUM AFTER YOUR CAMPAIGN

Some of you have just kicked off your campaign, some of you are deep in the trenches of it, and others are rounding the corner toward the end. No matter where you are in the process, it's never too early to begin thinking about and planning for what you'll do next. Here are five crucial strategies that will help you sustain the momentum after your campaign.

1. Use the pulpit to communicate the role of community. It's critical to communicate a clear vision, so be sure about what you want and then communicate that to the church. Many pastors and leaders make the mistake of giving too many messages, thus not effectively communicating any of them. According to Acts 5:42, God has called us to spread the Gospel in the temple courts and from house to house. So make the message of small group ministry a distinct and unmistakable one at your church. And don't be afraid to use the sermons to do so. If your pastor doesn't cast a vision for groups, then people won't understand what the groups are about and the direction your church is headed.

An easy and great way to incorporate this into sermons throughout the year is by telling stories and sharing testimonials from small groups. One small group champion regularly meets with his Senior Pastor to share small group stories. If you are the small group champion in your church, you have the responsibility to feed stories to your senior pastor each week. These stories will motivate people to action, thus fostering more stories. To solicit feedback from an even wider circle, try asking for stories in your bulletin or newsletter.

2. Provide natural next steps. Congregations and small group members respond if you chart the course by providing proven suggestions for the next steps toward growth. Do this throughout the campaign and throughout the year. Don't leave people guessing about what's next.
You can provide "next steps" by piloting or test-driving the next campaign. Use this as an opportunity to launch more groups. Celebrate your current or previous hosts, and then recruit the next phase of leaders. Ask each group to hold an open house and invite more people to come for the next series.

3. Prepare to launch new small group teams as needed. After overseeing the 40 Days campaign, no doubt the director or champion is tired. If so, recruit and develop a new leader to ensure that you sustain your small group ministry energy and motivation.

Also, keep in mind that some small group leaders will want to continue, and some will want to move on. Either way, this is an incredible opportunity to build your team. Be sure to thank the leaders for their service and release them, but ask them to prayerfully consider continuing on. This will give people the opportunity to re-energize and give you more than they had before.

As you recruit and cultivate new leadership, consider the six "L's." These are characteristics every leader should possess:

1. They are a **leader** of leaders.
2. They are **loyal** to the Senior Pastor.
3. They are **listening** to God and have a growing relationship with him.
4. They have a **life** that is available to be used by God.
5. They **love** community and are involved in it.
6. You **like** them and enjoy being with them.

Ask God to reveal the right leadership to you, and then help the new leaders build their teams.

4. Plan your work and work your plan. Incorporate the purposes into everything you do. Develop a one-year plan, in which the purposes are studied, cultivated, and practiced. Try using our one-year purpose planner (in appendix) to help you align the purposes with curriculum and sermon series.

This planner can serve as an example to you, or you can use it verbatim.

Now that you have a plan, you have to work it. Think about the key strategies you want to implement throughout the year. When do you need to hold host trainings? When is the best time for staff and leadership retreats? What future promotions could use stories from your current campaign? To simplify the process, use a one-year strategic timeline. This will help you select strategies for each month of the year to coincide with your campaigns and curriculum and sermon series. Now you have no excuse for not having a one-year plan, and then working that plan to achieve success.

5. Leverage technologies for communications. In our current technologically advanced world, there's no reason not to be on the pulse of your congregational and small group needs and in touch as a community. Simply use technology to enhance and broaden your communication. You can do this by:

- Getting stories to an even wider audience by putting them in an electronic newsletter.
- Using electronic surveying resources, such as www.zoomerang.com or www.surveymonkey.com, to capture group information overnight.
- Getting an online database to keep your contact information up to date so you can send out information regularly.
- Using video to clearly communicate the message of community.
- Using streaming video for devotionals.
- Using DVD teaching to equip and empower your coaches to do the training rather than you.
- Using Web technology to share tools and post testimonials.
- Using a tele-conferencing resource, such as www.freeconference.com, to conduct training.

Try one or all of these possibilities, and you'll be amazed at your progress, insight, and growing momentum.

So whether you've just begun your campaign or you're finishing the final stretch, these are five strategies you will definitely want to take advantage of. They are proven methods for sustaining all that you've done to create such a powerful momentum. And you'll want to keep going, because God has only begun working in the lives of your community.

NO TIME. NO RESOURCES. NO LEADERS.
FOUR TRICKS TO LAUNCH SOMETHING BIG WITH SMALL RESOURCES.

After 9/11, President Bush challenged Americans to participate in a national candle lighting ceremony and to ask God for help to get through the tragedy. The response was incredible. Days later I walked through my neighborhood and suggested to neighbors that we do something like this in our neighborhood as an evangelistic outreach and to show what happens when communities work together.

I first called men and women in my church who led Bible studies and got them on board. I then allied with a couple of women on the block who are the hub of information and networks. They directed me to the Moms in Touch group and introduced me to the PTA president of the elementary school. Through the PTA, I connected with the principal and significant businesses that donated money for the event. The principal led me to a group of enthusiastic teachers who helped me figure out the logistics of the event and introduced me to the junior and senior high principals who also lent support.

One day I walked into the local junior high and asked if they'd like to help out. They immediately suggested I make an announcement to the entire school. This junior high principal also turned me on to the junior high PTA network. The president sent out a blanket email that reached 80 percent of the parents of the junior high students.

Then someone connected me to the police and fire departments. We had the color guard. We had the Girl Scouts and the Boy Scouts all dressed.

This happened in a matter of 36 hours. Through this web of relationships, 1300-1500 folks came to this one event. The power of small groups to mobilize is an incredible force. This is the most transferable illustration that I can give you of how to find an unlimited harvest of leaders.

What did I do that is transferable to any small group ministry?

1. I found natural leaders.
Once I found a few leaders, those leaders found other leaders. I just had a few hours and no time to singularly produce this event. I had to rely on other natural leaders in the community to make connections. It's advantageous to do this because they already have a personal connection with people with whom they're comfortable. They've got a network.

2. I worked with affinity groups that already existed.
Affinity groups have trust. And trust gets you access. It also gets you loyalty, buy-in, credibility, and influence. As a volunteer who has limited time and resources, especially if you don't have a senior pastor involved, you don't have the pulpit to be able to leverage this. So you have to work with existing networks that have influence in order to get people to say yes.

3. I worked with existing activities that happened before I showed up.
Moms in Touch, PTA, community Bible study, and daytime ladies studies provide some of the best leader training resources that are out there. Yet sometimes we are so presumptuous to think that that we are the ones who are going to train all of our leaders. Remember you can find already trained leaders from existing relationships in every community in everyday places.

4. I worked the crowd.
I didn't just go to the principals, but I also went to the teachers and the kids. The most strategic place you can work is the crowd. Be vocal at your church's weekend services to get the crowd to move to the next step and speak to their longing to belong to community. Challenge them to come to a place where they can get that.

BUILDINGLIFETOGETHER

SMALL GROUPS HELP BELIEVERS FULFILL THE GREAT COMMISSION TOGETHER

"We are like sheep, and sheep are dumb," admitted a small group member in their recent meeting. Another member of the group took offense, "Are you calling me dumb?" Obviously, this was one of the sharper sheep. I would have been offended too. I'm not dumb, but I am a sheep, and sheep need to be led.

Many pastors and church leaders have bought into this idea. "How can my people lead when they need to be led?" Typically, when pastors think of leaders in the church, often our thoughts gravitate toward 1 Timothy 3. As the shepherd of our flocks, our job is to watch over our sheep and protect them from the wolves of heresy, egotism, and multi-level marketing. We take great pains in certifying "qualified" leaders or else groups will only be led into trouble.

The problem is that the harvest is plentiful, the workers are few, and our certification and training processes have created a tremendous bottleneck. "If only more qualified leaders would walk through the doors of my church, then these problems would be solved." But, is this the mission that we are called to?

I believe that we have made this way too complicated. The Great Commission commands every believer to "Go and make disciples of all nations…" (Matthew 28:19-20). How are we equipping every believer in our congregations to make disciples? Our excuse is often that our members need more training before they can lead others. We continue to train, and the harvest continues to wither.

At New Life Christian Center in Turlock, California, we have found that fulfilling the Great Commission is as easy as putting a Lifetogether study like the Experiencing Christ Together series in the hands of any member who is willing to gather a circle of friends. The step by step curriculum guides the discussion. There's even leadership training and a video commentary to help the leader/host prepare for the lesson. The host doesn't need to be a Bible scholar.

BUILDINGLIFETOGETHER

The Bible scholars are on the video.

Since each lesson balances the five biblical purposes, the health of the group increases from week to week. Every week group members grow in their ability to connect with God and with each other, to learn and do God's Word and to reach out to others. By simply following along with the study, the group can become what we desire for it to be.

With the support of experienced small group leaders and staff, the new host is empowered to "go and make disciples…" They are no longer sitting on the sidelines wondering what part they have to play in building God's Kingdom. They are living in obedience to the last words that Christ gave to His Church. And, group members are coming to Christ and being discipled in their groups.

When questions come up or problems surface, an experienced leader who is building a relationship with each new small group host/leader is right there to help the group navigate the issue and solve the problem. For first time "coaches" and mentors, a curriculum like Coaching Lifetogether takes some of the fear out of mentoring other leaders. The key to knowing the group is to know the leader. As this relationship grows between coaches or community leaders and the group host/leader, then the leader grows and the group grows.

For some pastors, this might seem too out of control. Please understand that I am not advocating chaos, just momentum. You cannot sideline character in the process of building groups. But rather than rejecting "unqualified" leaders, why not help them step by step to become qualified? If they are teachable, you are well on your way to developing a great leader. If they are unteachable, then it really doesn't matter how long they've been a Christian. They probably won't become a good leader.

The harvest is plentiful, and the workers are, well, sitting in our pews. How can we help to get them in the game?

EVANGELISM EXPLOSION
HOW GOD USED ONE SMALL GROUP MINISTRY'S "PROBLEM" TO REACH A COMMUNITY

Finding leaders is an ongoing bottleneck in the process of growing any church or ministry. Having too many leaders is rarely a problem. But that's exactly the situation that Overlake Church in Redmond, Washington, faced as they launched a small group movement.

"People in the Seattle area like to congregate around issues and ideas," says Dean Orrico, Senior Associate Pastor over Connect Ministries. For this reason, the leadership expected they would have no problems finding members for their small groups. Their concern was: Could they find enough leaders?

In an attempt to summon leaders, Senior Pastor Rick Kingham told church members that Overlake really needed "hosts"—people to make group members feel welcome and comfortable—more than leaders.

A huge percentage of the members responded to their pastor's call to host a group. Soon they realized they had so many hosts that they would only be able to fill each group with three members.

Instead of being greeted with a backlash of concern, hosts responded by going to their own neighborhoods and work places, families and friends to make their own groups. Because people didn't count on church members to fill the groups, Orrico explains, "It turned into a very evangelistic movement … more so than we'd even hoped."

Story after story confirms that every step along the way has had eternal value. One host invited a neighbor to attend his new group. This man, in his 80s, shared that he'd been in a small group many years before. However, it had been so long that the former members had all either moved, left the church or passed away, including his wife who had died four years prior.

There was no one left in his group. He had been coming to church alone for the last four years and sitting by himself. In tears, he told his new group, "It's so good to know that I don't have to be alone any more."

It's been amazing to see how God turned a "problem" of too many hosts into a life-changing experience for so many.

PUT PEOPLE INTO MINISTRY, NOT ON COMMITTEES

Rick Warren

Think about it: the most valuable asset people can give to your church is their time. If a man or woman comes to me and says, "Pastor, I have four hours a week to give to the church in ministry," the last thing I'm going to do is put him or her on some committee.

Committees discuss while ministries do. Committees argue while ministries act. Committees maintain while ministries minister. Committees talk and consider while ministries serve and care. Committees discuss needs while ministries meet needs. We must minimize maintenance in order to maximize time for ministry.

Maintenance is church work: budgets, buildings, and organizational matters. Ministry is the work of the church. The more people you involve in maintenance decisions, the more you keep them from ministry.

We have no committees at Saddleback. We do, however, have 150 different lay ministries. Our paid staff does the maintenance, and our lay ministers appreciate that the time they volunteer is given to actual ministry.

In streamlining your structure, it's better not to vote on ministry positions. There are several good reasons for this:

- It avoids personality contests and attracting people who are only interested in power or prestige.
- It allows new ministries time to develop slowly, out of the public spotlight.
- It allows new members a chance to get involved more quickly.
- It makes removal easier should people fail in a ministry.

Not voting on ministry positions also allows you to respond more quickly to the Holy Spirit's leading. Once a woman came to me and said, "We need a prayer ministry."

I said, "I agree. You're it."

She said, "Don't I have to be elected or go through some approval process?" She had imagined having to jump through all kinds of hoops first.

I said, "Of course not. Just announce a formation meeting in the bulletin and start it." She did.

You shouldn't have to vote on whether or not a person can use the gifts God has given him or her in the Body of Christ. I'm sure you realize how radical this approach is. In the typical church, members handle the maintenance (administration) of the church, and the pastor is supposed to do all the ministry. No wonder the church can't grow!

Copyright © 2009 Pastor.com. Used by permission.

SESSION 4
PRODUCE HEALTHY SMALL GROUPS THAT PRODUCE HEALTHY SMALL GROUP MEMBERS

Purpose of Ministry

1. **Begin** with the end in mine – what is Health?
   - Define success - What are we trying to produce at the end of the day?
   - Cast that vision very clearly- have everyone fill out a health assessment — *for you & grp.*
   - Do a gap analysis - out of 15 categories, come up with one goal

2. **Create** combined structure from the bottom up. Get it, Got it, Give it away.
   - Two things that God calls us all to do, not just the Great Commandment but also the Great Commission — *Serve together, Party's etc.*
   - Put a Ministry Plan together

3. **Curriculum** is more vital than you know.
   - Help small groups figure out what curriculum to do next
   - Individuals will be transformed over time by going six weeks on each of the purposes

4. **Launch** 'em & Lead them for life.
   - Church wide campaign
   - 40 Days of community helps connect the rest of your congregation
   - Individuals will be transformed over time by going six weeks on each of the purposes

we need balance w/ serving

5. **Align** church wide programs and resources.
   - ☐ Sermon alignment series with the small group curriculum
   - ☐ Bridge the holidays with a curriculum

6. **New leader** training coaching expectations are vital – class, campaigns and rally's.
   - ☐ Coach and train your leaders for life
   - ☐ Empower the groups to discover their individual shape for ministry through small groups and through Class
   - ☐ Develop their gift for life

7. **Focus** on the hard stuff.
   - ☐ Evangelism, ministry, etc.
   - ☐ Cast vision for people to express personal and group and corporate evangelism
   - ☐ Cast vision for doing group serving projects once a month or once a quarter.

8. **Select** a Core curriculum
   - ☐ Help them fulfill what God wants
   - ☐ Coach and cast vision that will challenge them

9. **Measure** success against biblical Health.
   - ☐ To cultivate greater depth in their relationship with Christ and helping them surrender more of their heart and life to him developmentally, not overnight but over time
   - ☐ If you want health and balance, we have got to break it down so that people are in relationships one on one, not one on man

10. **Secret** of Healthy Small Groups'.
    - ☐ Meet on a weekly basis, as is the model of the early church, where they met at temple courts and house-to-house and you'll double the relative amount of spiritual transformation and life change in any one of their lives
    - ☐ Manifest all five purposes deep in the heart and the life and ultimately in the community that wraps around every one of those Christian lives

- **Next steps from this session**
  Step 1. Write a few reflections on the teaching of this session

THE GROUP THAT SERVES TOGETHER GROWS TOGETHER
FIVE WAYS TO HELP TASK-ORIENTED GROUPS THRIVE

Setting up task groups is a great way to develop a growing number of faithful volunteers in almost any area of ministry. A task group is distinct in that it isn't just a traditional fellowship-building group or a team of people simply fulfilling a task. By definition, task groups attempt to accomplish both fellowship and ministry at the same time.

The principle mission of a task group is to set aside a 30-45-minute group time to develop the spiritual and relational life of each team member. People tend to join a group because of the task they want to work on, but ultimately they will stay because of the mutual caring among the group members. Being intentional about developing the sense of community through a designated group time strengthens and improves the overall health of the ministry.

Most of the principles used to develop effective traditional small groups can be transferred to working with task-oriented groups. However, several features will especially enhance the development of task groups:

1. Encourage groups to meet before or after their serving time. No matter how frequent the serving opportunity (whether once per week or once per quarter), add a community dimension to each meeting.

2. Monitor task-group curriculum selection and usage. To begin with, use simple, open-ended questions, such as those found in Nav-Press's *201 Questions*. Evolve to using an uncomplicated small-group curriculum. For instance, group members could respond to discussion questions after reading a short passage from a *Serendipity Bible* or *Life Application Bible*.

3. Develop a sense of *teammates* versus *soulmates*. People who join task groups generally have a primary commitment to the task and a secondary commitment to the people. Creating a teammate atmosphere helps everyone recognize that this group is different from the two-hour women's or couples' Bible study. Task-group members should accept and enjoy the fact that they have gathered in order to do something.

4. Make the task a means to a greater end. Ultimately, changed lives is our goal. Over 50 percent of those serving in a task group will never join a traditional fellowship group. Yet a task group is an excellent place to connect unconnected people. For this reason, encourage groups to form around any appropriate impassioned cause for which a qualified leader will emerge.

5. Provide ongoing leadership development. Leaders of task groups need regular support, training, troubleshooting help, and encouragement in order to lead over the long haul. Also, leaving an "open chair" (for the potential invited newcomer) in task group meetings will serve as the principle means of gathering the next generation of volunteers and leaders.

WHERE DO WE GO FROM HERE?
SEVERAL CHURCH LEADERS SHARE THEIR DO'S AND DON'TS ABOUT SUSTAINING THEIR 40 DAYS OF PURPOSE SMALL GROUPS

Much could be said from the trenches of the campaigns... But after listening to some of the most successful small group champions they all boil things down to a few do's and don'ts!

Their thoughts on the "Do's" are simple…

1. Do it again! "40 Days of Purpose is and was one of the most successful campaigns we have ever had in our church," Scott Mawdesley from Christ Fellowship Church, Florida. Many churches are repeating or reviewing the campaign and many are using the new Doing Lifetogether DVD Teaching Series the second time through. Gary Kendall from Indian Creek Church in Kansas said "We went through 40 Days of Purpose a year ago but our people need to be reminded year after year. The "Beginning Lifetogether" DVD series allows for our people to hear six of the best authors and speakers in the country and it's a great compliment to what I was teaching on the weekend. Best of all it's this Purpose Driven Group Resource, helps to take the purposes deeper every year. "I can see us doing this review of the purposes for the next few years."

2. Do a Survey – Before and after each of your small group series or key seasons of the year like September and January. This allows for a "check in" and then a "check up" on the health and strength of your leaders and their groups. That way you can measure the "levels" of life change that is happening or not. There are several surveys from Lifetogether you can use to benchmark your small group leaders, groups an even the entire ministry's health.

   a. **LifeTogether Health Assessment -** Based on the five purposes of the church. You can send this via e-mail to your entire church or to your small groups – then have them all do this at the end of each series. This is a great New Years survey as well.

   b. **Small Group Host / Leader Survey -** This is a great new leader application and provides a great pulse of the general maturity, experience and training needs of your new hosts and leaders. There is a pre and post survey. The Pre Survey is about their qualifications and experience. The Post Survey is about their willingness to continue. This survey can do ten times more work than even the best small group staff.

   c. **Small Group Stories Survey -** Is a great way to collect stories after each series or even for sermon illustrations down the road. Senior Pastors will love this new survey.

"Email Connection to your Leaders is vital to the launching and leading of a healthy Small Group Ministry" says Jeff Edwards from Scottsdale Bible Church in Arizona. We sent weekly emails to our leaders with a story attached to each one.

3. **Do Sermon Alignment Again in the Fall!**
Aligning the Small Group Studies with the weekend series is on of the most powerful ways to assimilate the largest number of people into groups. It takes at least 2-3 series to get 100 percent of your average weekend attendance but you can do it. Kenton Beeshore at Mariners Church in Irvine California, used the fellowship series "Connecting with God's Family") and put 90 percent into groups during a spring campaign. He had a good start but still put 3500 new people after one six week series. This was a perfect setup to fall capital campaign where they exceeded their goals by 20 percent.

You can't do this all year long although Mike Meeks at East Lake Community Church in San Diego feels its something you can do 2-3 times a year. He started off doing 40 Days of Purpose then went into the number one Lifetogether follow up series to the campaign titled "Connecting with God's Family" the fellowship series. This series helps to ensure your groups stay connected beyond the first 40 Days. Now Mike is finishing the worship series titled "Surrendering your Heart for God's Pleasure" which can be a great kick off series as well. One staff member said "the place is buzzing every weekend." Kevin Odor at Canyon Ridge, in Las Vegas is using this series as a fall kick off after doing 3 other Doing LifeTogether studies.

Alignment isn't just about sermons and small groups but also several other key areas as well. Now that there is a **Youth DVD and study guides series**. Josh, the Youth Pastor at Overlake Church in Seattle, WA said, "we can follow right along with the rest of the church."

Also the Sunday Worship Services can use the **Lifetogether Worship Series** from Maranatha and Lifetogether. This has helped to increase the size and shape of our heart for worship as a church.

John Bodin the Small Group Pastor at Central Christian Church is excited about Introducing a "Church wide gift education and motivation" with a 40 Days of Purpose Campaign using the ministry serving curriculum from the Doing Lifetogether series titled "**Developing your SHAPE for ministry.**" All hands on deck will mean all kinds of discoveries.

4. **Do Plan for What's Next -** Sometimes it takes a while but most Senior Pastors come to realize that resourcing their Small Group Ministry and the development of their leaders is vital to the long term success of the 40 Day effort – otherwise that's all it will be, a 40 Day flash in the pan. The Peoples Church in Nashville launched 60 groups during the campaign but lost most of them because of their

lack of planning for what's next. Their small group Pastor said he wished he knew how vital it was to plan for the long haul. Expectations on the front side and encouragement on the back side can make a huge difference. If only they had introduced the next series on week four or even five they might have saved 50 percent of their groups.

Most churches that had success from one series to the next offered one or max two series to their Group leaders. Most groups are very open especially since they had such a positive experience with 40 Days. Saddleback is recommending the James Series from Rick Warren which is a great study or the Foundations material that reviews the Doctrines of the Faith which is another excellent choice. If either of those two don't meet your needs, the six week discipleship series titled "**Growing to be like Christ**" is one of our best studies and a great follow up series to Easter. This is a great series to do sermon alignment in order to start the fall season strong. Kent Odor from Canyon Ridge Church in Las Vegas, Nevada sees this as a great way to get their 200+ groups in the word and going deeper in their walks with Christ.

The next sequence in the series if you get off to a good start in mid January is to follow it with the evangelism series titled "**Sharing Your Life Mission Everyday.**" The six teachers include Doug Fields, Erwin McManus, Bruce Wilkinson, Alvin Bibbs from Willow Creek, and Todd Wendorff one of the co-authors of the series. This series will prepare your people to share their faith like no other series and hold them accountable each week to sharing their faith. Tom Mullins, Senior Pastor at Christ Fellowship saw a 40 percent increase in their weekend Easter attendance after their groups went through the first four sessions. It was a remarkable response like nothing they had ever seen. 1500 new families attended the church that weekend.

5. **Do Story Telling -** Every weekend in illustrations, bulletin announcements, e-newsletters, testimonies, etc. have the stories of how God is transforming lives in community everywhere. This will show your people that small groups aren't not just a flash in the pan or another program that came in and out of town. One church launched over 100 groups and proceeded to have them reduce after a six month period. "Everybody went back to business as usual". Somebody has to be the vision caster, the bell ringer or the champion. All the better if it's the senior pastor but until they become like Rick Warren at Saddleback, keep waving the flag.

Overtime, you will be able to naturally challenge the congregation to "get connected" or more importantly "open your home" to host a new six week series. You can like Jimmy Davidson in Abingdon Virginia, see hundreds of people step up to connect in groups and open their homes in waves that never need to stop. The question is will you continue to share the stories and cast the vision at the end of each series or at least every six weeks?

10 WAYS TO SUSTAIN YOUR NEW SMALL GROUPS

Help For What's Next After A 40 Day Campaign

Your church has been on a spiritual roll with the 40 Days of Purpose campaign. Everyone's excited, but you're actually worried: What will happen to these new small groups once 40 Days is over? *No need to fret. With these 10 tips, you can sustain and strengthen your small groups from Day 41 onward.*

1. Ask Your Leaders, "What's Next?"

Contact your small group leaders to thank them for their participation and ask some quick questions. Through a phone conversation or email, get the "Four P's" of Feedback:

Praise: What happened in their group for which they are grateful to God? Let them share stories of how God has been changing lives. When they relive that excitement, they will become energized about leading another small group.
Problem: What one problem did they encounter? It might be curriculum choice, a difficult person, or group dynamics. Whatever the problem, let them talk and feel supported by you.
Plans: What is your group doing next? If they don't have a plan, share with them what other groups are doing and discuss what would best fit their group.
Prayer: Any prayer requests? In that moment, pray for it. To show your earnest concern, follow up with an email in which you write out a prayer for them.

2. Schedule Leaders Celebration.

Rally all the new and existing leaders for a time of honor, strategy, praise, and vision. The best place to have a celebration is in a key lay leader's home, though you can do it at church after a Sunday service You and other key staff should be there.

This is a time to hear leaders' stories and celebrate what God's been doing. This is also another opportunity to thank leaders. One great way is by sharing "insider news" regarding the next sermons series or some of the next steps the church is taking. When the senior pastor or small groups pastor shares this news, it is even more meaningful. It brings leaders into the fold and makes them feel included.

Many churches forget to celebrate, so hosts celebrate hosts—rather than church leaders celebrating the hosts. Leadership needs to say, "Well done, good and faithful servant."

3. Prayerfully Identify a New Small Group Champion.

After overseeing the 40 Days campaign, no doubt the director or champion is tired and on the edge of burnout, and for good reason. Recruit and develop a new leader to ensure you sustain your small group ministry energy and motivation.

How do you know what type of person you're looking for? The person should have five qualities:

1. Loyal to the Senior Pastor
2. Part of the small groups community
3. The gift and experience of leadership
4. Character that is above reproach
5. A growing and deepening relationship, with God

Ask God to reveal the right leadership to you. When you do find the right individual and they agree to help you bridge 40 Days to the future, send your other champion on vacation so they'll return ready to lead again.

4. Plan Your Work, and Work Your Plan.
This is where you ask, "Lord, where do you want us to go?" And then obediently go where he leads. Get a "spiritual pulse" of your Small Group Ministry by taking the feedback from your staff, from your host meetings, and from your celebration, and come up with a six-week to six-month tentative calendar. If you don't think through the next six weeks, you risk losing a lot of momentum. It's like when you plant a new tree in your back yard, you have to put a stake next to it for at least six months so that it will eventually thrive. The calendar is the stake.

If you're ending the 40 Days campaign near the holidays, make sure you consider those breaks. The holidays have the potential to break up 50 percent of your groups, unless you think through carefully how to manage the process. Consider shorter curriculum during holiday times or preaching on 40 Days of Purpose-related themes to keep people connected with and enthused about small groups.

5. Preview, Select, and Promote Your New Small Group Series.
A six-week study gives people only a taste of the 5 biblical purposes. Folks, though, need to be transformed by the purposes, and that happens only over time. So start previewing curriculum that will do just that. (A logical place to start previewing the available curriculum is at www.lifetogether.com where you'll find many curricula written by different authors.)

Once you've selected your new curriculum, you've got to promote it. If you should choose a curriculum from Purpose Driven, we have provided many resources that are available for you, including order forms for the curriculum that you can make available at church. This way, instead of sending individuals out to get their own materials, you can collectively order the materials. This requires some upfront capital from church, but purchasing these—and then having people pay for them when they pick them up—makes it easier for people to stay connected.

6. Access Important Resources and Tools.
Many great tools are available online. Have your leaders sign up for Lifetogether Today at www.Lifetogether.com. It is a free weekly newsletter that features articles and other resources from Lifetogether. They can also sign up to receive free weekly video training via the "Small Group University" video emails and you can sign up for "The Pastor Show" and "The Small Group Show," free weekly videos by Lifetogether to help train and equip pastors. Also at Lifetogether.com the Small Group University section with many downloadable and printable resources for small group leaders. Another great site is www.zoomerang.com. It's a low-cost

resource that provides all kinds of questions to ask your leaders regarding their small groups' future plans.

Another website is www.smallgroups.com This site has great ideas, stories, and strategies for small groups and small group champions.

7. Offer End-of-Year Leader/Host Training.
Rally your leaders for a time of fun, fellowship, and small-group vision—and make sure your pastoral leadership is present You can either send out nice invitations or casual emails. To ramp up the excitement, do something creative—like a cookie exchange or a White Elephant party. If you throw the party on a Saturday morning or Sunday afternoon, you'll wind up with a two-and-a-half or three-hour block of time.

If you don't use training material, use the time to listen to and love on them. Go over the "Four P's" (Praises, Problems, Plans, Prayers) to get your conversation going. Give your leaders plenty of opportunities to share with other group leaders. Often, small group leaders share similar concerns and are able to work out their problems together. From those conversations, you'll also learn where you need to spend time training.

8. Leverage the Weekend Services.

The greatest communication tool that you have in your church is the weekend services. If the pastor isn't casting a vision for groups, people aren't going to understand what the groups are about and the direction the church is headed.

This is also a great time to share with the congregation what God is doing in your small groups. One small group champion regularly met with his Senior Pastor to share small group stories. The pastor would often use these stories in sermons to generate interest in small groups. (To get stories from an even wider circle, solicit stories in your bulletin or newsletter.)

9. Identify, Train, and Develop a Coaching Staff.

Use the same five characteristics of small group champions to identify coaches. A great place to look is at the people already doing the job--without the title. Go after people who have hosted, had a positive 40 Day experience, and have proven gifts of leadership.

One technique for finding coaches is a "leadership connection." In real time, gather all your leaders together. While they are together, ask them to nominate a "relative" coach who could shepherd the rest of them, someone whom they respect. Then you can ask that coach who he or she thinks would be a great future coach. In essence, the team chooses the coach for the team. Many people who receive this nomination feel honored, making it more difficult for them to turn down.

10. Attend a Purpose Driven Small Group Conference.

Purpose Driven offers some regional conferences around the country on leadership issues. We are also launching a national conference next June. The conference is geared towards Senior Pastors, Small Group Pastors and Champions to help you put some processes in place. You'll come away with a plan for how you are going to implement Purpose Driven small groups in your church.

COACHING THAT WORKS

So, once you've got your members connected, what do you do with them? At New Life Christian Center in Turlock, California, our small groups went from connecting 30 percent of our adults to connecting 125 percent in just six months with the help of Lifetogether Coaching Program. Many churches have experienced this kind of success through a 40 Day Campaign or their own campaign. But, once you have them, how do you keep them?

According to Carl George, there are two reasons that most groups don't make it: The lack of an effective coaching structure or the presence of a neurotic personality. Effective coaching can go a long way in solving both problems.

But, what does effective coaching look like? Most seminary-trained pastors' idea of coaching is training meetings and reporting for the sake of quality control. Hosts and group leaders are divided into geographical areas and are assigned a coach who periodically inspects their group and trains them. The problem with this sort of coaching is that no one likes to do it or have it done to them. It simply doesn't work.

What works looks very different from the typical management structure. Consider these three areas in your coaching structure:

First of all, consider **Relationships over Region**. How many churches do your members drive past in order to attend your church? If location was everything, then our church would not attract people from a 40 mile radius. This is also true for the relationship between coaches and group leaders. Geography may seem like a simple management solution. But, it is simply ineffective.

In assigning group leaders to coaches, our Small Group Community Leaders did something much different from geographical division. (Some churches use the term "Division Leaders." We feel like "division" is not a good thing to encourage in the church. Community Leaders are our leaders of coaches). We conducted an NBA-style draft. I gave then a list of our experienced group leaders, then they went around the table and chose who they already knew to be on their team. Then, we did the same with our new hosts and leaders. This wasn't a perfect system, since there were some that none of us knew. But, it did give us a leg up on coaching by focusing on relationship over region.

In a recent Community Leader meeting, someone raised the issue that some of leaders never returned phone calls. The others nodded in agreement. I asked them, "Whose calls do you return?" They indicated that they all returned calls that were important to them to people who were important to them. I, then, challenged them to become that person to their leaders. Our Community Leaders and coaches had no problem staying in contact with hosts and leaders that they already had a relationship with. The problem came from leaders who didn't know

BUILDING**LIFE**TOGETHER   57

them. As relationships are built, coaching becomes what it should to support leaders and sustain groups.

Secondly, emphasize **Encouragement over Enforcement**. Years ago one of my coaches told me, "When I go out and visit groups, I feel like I'm your spy." At the time, she was exactly right. Every pastor wants to know what is happening in their groups. Many coaching structures include the component of group visits for the sake of maintaining quality control. While the quality of the group is important, the relationship between the coach and leader is the best way to get there. If the coach's visit is perceived as an evaluation by the principal, it's probably not going to do much for the relationship.

Rather than visiting groups with clipboard in hand, coaches should visit groups with the purpose of building up the leader to the group. The group needs to know that the coach believes in the leader. And, it certainly does a lot for the relationship between leader and coach, when the coach visits to encourage and support rather than inspect and enforce. As their relationship develops and trust is built, the leader will feel confident in sharing any issues going on in the group.

Think about it. When people are invited to become leaders because "anyone can do it," a certain amount of pressure accompanies the invitation. What if a host starts a group and they soon discover that there are things they can't do? They may feel like a failure. "Anyone can do it, except me." It's the feeling that newlyweds get when the honeymoon is over and love hasn't conquered all. If they go to talk to someone, they might just have to admit that the whole thing now seems like a big mistake. How many groups fail, not for the lack of a coaching structure, but because the new leader felt uncomfortable talking to their coach about a problem?

Thirdly, place **Their Needs over Your Notes**. What questions are your leaders asking? Answer the questions they are asking rather than giving answers to questions they're not asking. Last summer, I was given the task of getting our preschool son ready for swim lessons one afternoon. I had located his swim diaper, swim trunks, cover up, flip flops and basically everything he needed except for his sun screen. I couldn't find it anywhere. My wife called and told me where the swim diapers were, where they swim trunks were, where the cover up was, and where his flip flops were…all of the things that I had already found. All the while I was trying to ask her about the sun screen. Then, her cell phone died. She told me what she knew, but she didn't tell me what I needed to know. What do your leaders need to know? Ask them. Send out a survey. Don't assume.

I was doing a series of conference calls for churches doing 40 Days campaigns. I was one among several teachers on various calls. During one of the last calls, I just opened up the whole hour for questions. What we discovered was that the leaders on the conference call asked questions about all of the items on our agenda without ever seeing it. The conversation was highly engaging since we were directly answering the questions they were asking. Another teacher covered the same outline in lecture format, then opened it up for questions. No one asked a single question. Had they're questions all been answered? Possibly. Had the lecture stifled their interaction? Most likely.

Assume that your leaders are highly intelligent, motivated individuals who are doing hand to hand combat in the small group trenches. Give them what motivates them. Teach them the skills they need to learn. Offer the information they need. How do you find that out? Ask them.

Coaching built on relationships, encouragement and your leaders' needs is coaching that works. If you don't believe me, then just try it the other way around. Then, again, don't. The best thing that any coach can do is figure out how many ways he or she can serve their leaders. Coaching is serving at a higher level.

MENTOR YOUR COACHES AND THEIR LEADERS

3 levels of Spiritual Mentoring that will keep your leaders in the game.

Supervising leaders face burn out and fatigue just as any uncared-for small group leader does.

As a pastor or staff member, one of your jobs is to focus on the needs of your leadership coaches and supervisors to ensure that they want to stick around and help you turn spiritual seekers into multiplying "shepherds." Often just a little extra effort will pay off big. Let's take a look at three main areas:

1. "Who Are You?"

This focuses on relationship and friendship. To develop a deeper relationship with your coaches:

a. Pray with them. Ask what you can pray for on their behalf.
b. Take a genuine interest in their family.
c. Write them notes of encouragement often.
d. Call them or send them cards on their birthdays or anniversaries.
e. Make sure you know their life story.
f. Make a point to have fun together.

2. "How Are You?"

This focuses on transparency and accountability. To help your coaches in their personal growth:

a. Share what God is teaching you-take them to Scripture.
b. Share personal struggles and victories.
c. Share the value of a assessing a group's "health" from your personal perspective.
d. Assess the health of the coach's groups together and then work up a "health plan."
e. Challenge and encourage your coaches to take their next spiritual steps.

3. "Where Can I Help You?"

The following focus on developing and equipping your coaches:

a. Go through a book together.
b. Do a lunch-hour solitude experience.
c. Do a prayer-walk together.
d. Pray and fast together.

SOMETIMES MINISTRY IS MESSY

If you take the risk to launch new small groups, it always ends up a little messy. One new small group leader once told that he and his live-in girlfriend were so excited about the 20 people they had coming to their group. We had no idea that she was his girlfriend and not his wife until he told us.

I ended up marrying the couple in a break-out room at Saddleback filled with their small group cheering them on. The couple was the most mature of the entire small group, so once I married them, we let them continue to lead the group. That same group had a baptism, with six of them being baptized by their spiritual shepherd. That group is still meeting almost seven years later. God is good!

The key question is, "What is the point of "40 Days of Purpose"? Or any spiritual or small group campaign for that matter? It's simply an organizing principle, program, and process to help the people in your church live healthy, balanced, Purpose Driven Lives.

It's not just about connecting people into community for the sake of community, but changing community *through* community in order to convert our culture for the sake of Christ.

SHAPING SHEPHERDS AND SHEEP
6 STEPS TO MENTOR YOUR LEADERS AND THEIR GROUPS.

A friend who was in charge of our men's ministry once said, "Some of these guys really don't want me coaching them; they don't want my help!"

"That's all right," I said, "If all these guys are living spiritually healthy lives, you can take it easy."

"But some aren't thriving spiritually," he said. "They need encouragement."

A coach's primary goal is to help leaders become fully mature in Christ. Colossians 1:28 says, "We are to proclaim him, admonishing every man and woman, and teaching every man with all wisdom that we may present every man or woman complete in Christ." Jesus desires that we grow deeper in our walk with him so we're prepared for the mission to which God has called us.

By mentoring small group leaders and their groups, we participate in the process of presenting every man and woman complete in Christ. This happens by helping them cultivate their spiritual health—even when it's an uphill battle.

The acronym **MENTOR** provides steps to help you guide your small group leaders to spiritual maturity.

Motivate them to find a spiritual partner. You might think you already are their spiritual partner, but realistically, you can't be every leader's partner. One of the greatest gifts you can give your leaders is another person who will help them move to the next step in their spiritual journey, including listening, encouraging, fellowshipping, and exhorting.

Gently remind your leaders that if they're going to lead in the church, they must grow in their faith. Then simply ask them who they would like to help them grow--this shifts the burden from you to them. You might periodically connect with the partners, but the bottom line is once they're connected, transformation follows.

Since it's often difficult to ask someone to be a partner, encourage them through the process and celebrate with them when they finally pair up. As soon as one leader is paired up, other leaders will be encouraged to pair up as well.

Encourage them to review the health assessment regularly. To help them identify the next step in their spiritual journey, guide them through a health assessment. These tools ask pointed questions about your spiritual journey and give guidelines for setting and achieving goals. Using a health assessment is a way of taking stock—understanding the areas in which you are strong, as well as the areas in which you need to grow. Don't be afraid to refer to the health assessment when meeting with your leaders. Ask them, "Remember when we walked through that health assessment? How are you doing in your weak areas?" or "How can I pray for your spiritual growth?"

You also might consider visiting your leaders' small groups and administering the health assessment to the entire group. This gives you the chance to see how the group is doing and ask the group where they want to grow. Groups usually thrive in fellowship and discipleship, but struggle when it comes to evangelism and serving. A health assessment builds group ownership as well as continuity and growth. Later, you can discuss the group's goals with your leader and help determine the next steps to achieve these goals.

Follow-up visits—at least every other month—help groups stay focused on spiritual maturity. When you visit, come early and pray with the leader, affirm the group, check in on their goals, and ask how you can pray for the group. Afterwards, debrief with the leader and express your gratitude for their service.

Never forsake gathering together. If the disciples never gathered in the upper room or pulled away from the crowds with Christ, where would the church be? In the same way, you need to get away with your leaders and study God's Word, because faith comes by hearing the Word of God.

Setting a time in which all leaders can meet together is often difficult, but try gathering in a home once a month. When you meet, make sure you have fun together. They'll look forward to regular gatherings if you laugh together, pray together, and "fill their cup" so they can leave recharged and energized. They will take that energy back to their groups.

Don't cancel a gathering if only three or five can come. Those that make it will talk about its positive effect and inspire others to join in next time. You can also send an e-mail to those who weren't there to tell them you missed them and invite them to the next meeting.

Consider meeting around key events on the small group calendar: before new small group curriculum is launched and after a small group session has ended. At these meetings, celebrate with them, show your gratitude, and talk about the strong and weak aspects of their group. Always end the evening by praying for each other.

Tell them what you sense God wants them to hear. When you're talking on the phone, typing a simple e-mail, or gathered in a huddle, make sure you speak the truth to them—both challenges and blessings. It's important that you love them as you lead them.

Express your gratitude and tell them what you sense God wants them to hear--perhaps by reading or writing a passage of Scripture. You may sense a special call for their life that they haven't sensed. Maybe they need to be reminded of their unique gifts that equip them to lead their groups. You may recognize a gift they haven't yet recognized--pointing it out boosts their confidence and gives them vision. Help them redirect their eyes from the day-to-day tasks to what God might have planned for them.

One-on-ones are vital. Most leaders receive little affirmation, though they're a vital part of your church's small group ministry. You need to spend time loving, honoring, and listening to them—this gives them a sense of purpose. When they hear you believe in them, they're reenergized to do their job well.

One-on-ones don't have to happen weekly, or even monthly; however, you should strive to meet every four to six weeks. Don't worry about meeting formally. There was a time in my life when I didn't have time to play basketball, so I put a basketball hoop up and invited leaders over to play. One time I took a road trip and brought a leader along with me. Recently, I received an e-mail from him that shared how touched he was by my friendship; he similarly touched my life. Making a connection with your leaders is second to a big event.

Release them to multiply their lives. Part of coming together is also going back out. We don't come together for the sake of coming together. We come together so that we can go back out and multiply our lives. This means that I'm not just building into the lives of these leaders and they're not just building into the lives of their members. We are sending them out to multiply.

A woman named Mary exemplifies this. She discipled many women: both new and mature believers. Her greatest joy was sending them out after years of mentoring. One evening a group of 1,500 believers gathered to honor Mary. I asked, "Who in this room has been mentored by Mary?" About 40 women stood up. Then I said, "Now look around the room. How many of you have been impacted by the spiritual lives of the women who are standing?" About another 150 people stood up. I said, "Look again. If you see a woman or man who has radically changed your life, I'd like you to stand." About another 200 people stood up.

Don't you want to have that kind of impact?

Mentoring is essential to multiplication. It's not just about studying the Bible and spiritual formation--it requires that you dream a future for your leaders. While releasing them is difficult, it's important to challenge them to be courageous enough to break apart—perhaps in pairs—for six weeks. Have them invite neighbors and friends to study. Once the season is over, a new leader will have been created from this group and members can go back to their old groups.

BE A CHAMPION TO REMEMBER
LIFETOGETHER'S BRETT EASTMAN RECALLS HOW HIS FIRST SMALL GROUP CHAMPION SHARED WORDS THAT MADE A LIFELONG IMPACT

Although I've championed small groups in several big churches over the past decade, and even though it's been almost twenty years since I led my first small group, I still remember the day I led my first group like it was yesterday.

My palms were sweating, and I thought my heart was going to thump right out of my chest. But even though I was terrified, I knew God was there with me. He knew exactly where I was and what the group needed. In just the first six weeks, the Holy Spirit managed to pull us together as a group and even motivated two guys to ask Christ into their lives.

I believe God sent me one person to help in that first experience: a guy named John. He was my Small Group Champion. He came alongside me to help me lead that group successfully.

He said a couple of things that really mattered. One, he said, "Brett, you can do it." This may seem silly, but I really didn't feel like I could do it. But when he shared his confidence in me and showed he believed in me, it gave me the confidence to lead well.

The second thing he said was, "I will help you." And he did. He was there for every question or concern I had—no matter how silly they now seem to me.

These two simple statements sum up well the role of a great Small Group Champion. If you are a Champion, I encourage you to make sure your Leaders know you believe in them and are there to help. If you are a Leader, take advantage of the support your Champion offers. Take it from me, the relationship will take you far.

BUILDING LIFE TOGETHER

COACHING LIFE-CHANGING LEADERS

By Bill Donahue & Greg Bowman

Everybody needs a coach—whether to help you plant a garden, build a home, improve a golf swing or lead a small group. The question is: What does coaching look like? How do we inspire, shepherd and develop leaders of groups so that they grow in wisdom, maturity and skills?

To help our coaches we have outlined 4 key practices for the oversight of leaders.

- **Modeling: Pursue Christ-likeness.** Grow in the life of full devotion you're inviting others to lead. Paul said, "Follow my example as I follow the example of Christ." (*1 Corinthians 11:1*). I remember when Ryan, now almost 16, was just about 4 years old. We were walking down Michigan Avenue in Chicago and I was holding his hand. But then I let go to pick up a large piece of paper in our path on the otherwise clean sidewalk. I threw it in a trash can and turned to grab Ryan's hand—but he was gone. For a split second I panicked. It was a busy street with lots of passersby. I turned around and discovered he was several feet behind me, picking up another piece of trash he had spotted. He threw it in the can and grabbed my hand. It struck me—he watches everything I do!

    We are always modeling whether we realize it or not. Coaches should pursue the Jesus way of life for their own benefit and growth, but must also be aware that leaders are looking to them—at least sometimes—to show the way and to live a life worth emulating. We inspire others when we pursue Christ. It is job one for Coaches.

- **Guiding: Shepherd Intentionally.** Guides are sometimes holy sages and mystical gurus—but that is not the image we want you to think of. Coaching is simply helping people take the next step on the journey. Sometimes it is a journey you have taken personally; other times it requires pulling out the map and saying, "let's head this way together." The point is being intentional, conscious that we have an opportunity to guide a leader toward growth, service, connection with Jesus, or to seize ministry opportunities that arise. Coaches help leaders identify and take their next step of spiritual growth. *"Patiently correct, rebuke and encourage your people."* (2 Timothy 4:2).

- **Envisioning: Dream Together.** "Don't lose sight of good planning and insight. Hang onto them, for they will fill you with life and bring you honor and respect." (Proverbs 3:21 NLT) Proverbs says, "When dreams come true there is life and joy." (13:12 NLT). It is one thing to cast vision to leaders—it is another thing to cast vision *for* them. Instead of using only "let's take the hill" vision casting, think of ways to help leaders see what God is doing in and through them. "Rita, I believe God is using you to deeply affect the lives of people in your group, even though we do not see all the fruit now. I watch you—you pray, use your shepherding gifts, bring fresh ideas, and speak loving truth to people. Imagine the payoff that will come from that—people will stand stronger and run the race better. Do not underestimate the power of God working in you!" That kind of talk will inspire people, not simply call them to action.

- **Equipping: Develop Skills.** "Their responsibility is to equip God's people to do his work and build up the church, the body of Christ." (Ephesians 4:12, NLT) Coaches are not expected to be skill trainers in the formal sense. But neither should they underestimate the ability they have to share wisdom and experiences with leaders, and to point them to train classes, books, messages, and experiences that will help them grow in effectiveness.

Think of yourself as a golf or tennis coach more than a football coach. Observe people as they lead and as they describe their ministry, and then speak into the situation. If you cannot help, get help. But simply sharing a personal success and a few ministry tips can go a long way. Always come prepared to offer something—a word, idea, insight, or a resource—to leaders when you meet them 1-on-1 or at a leader gathering. See yourself as an equipper that comes alongside leaders to offer help and support for ministry—either directly or though the gifts of others you know.

Don't give up on Coaching –it is relational work and therefore sometimes hard work. But the impact multiplies when a leader is impacted. The ripple effect at the group level goes on and on—far beyond your ability to see. So just stand back and smile, knowing that the seed you sow in a leader's life today will bear fruit in a group tomorrow. That's the blessing of coaching leaders.

To learn more about how to train and support Coaches in this role, pick up *Coaching Life-Changing Small Group Leaders* by Bill Donahue and Greg Bowman at lifetogether.christianbook.com. Published by Zondervan.

SESSION 6
CREATE A CULTURE THAT CELEBRATES YOUR LIFE TOGETHER

Become what you celebrate

Purpose of Worship

Worship is more than music! *Luke 15:3-6*

1. **Devine** your ideal culture — *If you aim for nothing, you'll hit it every time.*
   - ☐ Purpose – What does God say is the purpose of worship?
   - ☐ Process – ownership
   - ☐ Prayer -
   - ☐ Retreat -
   - ☐ Success -

   *Groups Gathered together!

2. **Redefine** your weekend Celebration
   Sunday is a weekly celebration of Community

3. **Create** memories & moments — *Partys - Concerts - canoeing etc!; - Serving!*

4. **Rally** your leaders on and off campus.
   Hosting LT, Coaching LT, Building LT

5. **Plan** your work and work your plan – Create a Small Group Ministry **Planning Process**
   - ☐ Purpose
   - ☐ Priorities
   - ☐ Plans
   - ☐ Progress - Celebrate

6. **Leverage** emerging technologies
   - ☐ Video
   - ☐ Survey
   - ☐ Database
   - ☐ Streaming video
   - ☐ DVD teaching and Training
   - ☐ Gutenberg Press
   - ☐ Newsletters
   - ☐ email –
   - ☐ Video interviews
   - ☐ Home crashers
   - ☐ High School
   - ☐ Web Training
   - ☐ Satellite
   - ☐ Telecoaching

7. __Model__ a heart of Celebration
   Hot seat, sushi, etc.

8. __Catalyze__ Small Group Worship – 5th Purpose
   How
   LT Worship Series
   Grow into it

9. __Create__ new hero's
   - Individuals
   - Staff dinner
   - Leaders always share on weekend

10. __Come__ Together Around Food
    - Small group dinner
    - 1st week social
    - Leadership lunch
    - Break bread Community
    - Small Group Worship – 5th Purpose

Next Step
① meeting in June w/ Leslie & Ricci & Allen
② Timeline Rollout

Next steps from this session
Step 1. Write a few reflections on the teaching of this session

_____
_____
_____
_____
_____

BUILD COMMUNITY THROUGH COMMUNION

Looking for a wonderful means of worshipping as a group? Why not lead your group in sharing the Lord's Supper? If you've never done this before, the idea certainly seems daunting, but here is a simple form by which your small group can share this sacrament. Of course, churches vary in their treatment of Communion so you may need to adapt these suggestions to your church's beliefs.

STEPS IN SERVING COMMUNION

1. Out of the context of your own experience, say something brief about God's love, forgiveness, grace, mercy, commitment, tenderheartedness or faithfulness. Connect your words with the personal stories of the group. For example, "These past few weeks I've experienced God's mercy in the way he untangled the situation with my son. And I've seen God show mercy to others of us here too, especially to Jean and Roger." If you prefer, you can write down ahead of time what you want to say.

2. Read 1 Corinithians 11:23-26*:
The Lord Jesus, on the night he was betrayed, took bread, and when he had given thanks, he broke it and said, "This is my body, which is for you; do this in remembrance of me." In the same way, after supper he took the cup, saying, "This cup is the new covenant in my blood; do this, whenever you drink it, in remembrance of me." For whenever you eat this break and drink this cup, you proclaim the Lord's death until he comes.

3. Pray silently, and pass the bread around the circle. While the bread is being passed, you may want to reflect quietly, sing a simple praise song, or listen to a worship tape.

4. When everyone has received the bread, remind them that this represents Jesus' broken body on their behalf. Simply state, "Jesus said, 'Do this in remembrance of me.' Let us eat together," and eat the break as a group.

5. Pray silently, and serve the cup. You may pass a small tray, serve people individually, or have them pick up a cup from the table.

6. When everyone has been served, remind them that the cup represents Jesus' blood shed for them. Simply state, "The cup of the new covenant is Jesus Christ's blood shed for you. Jesus said, 'Do this in remembrance of me.' Let us drink together." Then drink the juice in a group.

7. Conclude by singing a simple song, listening to a praise song, or having a time of prayer in thanks to God.

PRACTICAL TIPS IN SERVING COMMUNION

1. Prepare the elements simply, sacredly, and symbolically.

2. Be sensitive to timing in your meeting.

3. Break up pieces of cracker or soft break on a small plate or tray. Don't use large servings of bread or grape juice. You should think about using grape juice—and not wine—because wine can cause some people to stumble.

4. Have all of the elements prepared beforehand, and just bring them into the room or to the table when you are ready.

*Here are some other good Communion passages: Matthew 26:26-29, Mark 14:22-25, Luke 22:14-20, 1 Corinthians 10:16-21 or 1 Corinthians 11:17-34.

MODELING THE HEART OF CELEBRATION

One thing that has been severely underestimated in our churches is the importance of celebration. In the New Testament, Paul visited churches to hear what God was doing and to share what he had experienced of God on his missionary journeys. Our weekend services are the perfect opportunity for us to hear and share what God is doing in our own missionary journeys.

Romans 10:17 tells us that faith comes by hearing, and hearing by the Word of God. We need to hear about people who took steps of faith, came to Christ, or are studying God's Word for the first time. **Celebration allows us the chance to praise God for all he's done.**

Celebrating moves even further than that, though. **It also leads to evangelism, allows us to develop deeper levels of relationships, and helps to cast a vision.** Celebrating is a unique catalyst that can help your church accomplish numerous goals.

As you've launched your 40 Day campaign, you're probably seeing growth in your small group ministry. **We want to help you sustain that growth, rather than lose 50 to 75 percent of the groups that are started.** To do that, here's an acrostic to help you understand what's at the *heart* of celebration. By celebrating, you can nurture what God has begun.

A. HONOR WHAT GOD HAS DONE.

One way to honor what God has done is to affirm and thank the people he used to do his work. That's why it's critical to give your congregation an opportunity to say thank you to the campaign hosts and leaders. It's even more crucial that your senior pastor and key leaders spearhead this acknowledgement. Take time during a weekend service to ask the campaign leaders to stand up and be recognized. Invite your campaign director onstage and present him or her with flowers or a gift certificate.

Another great sensory way to mark what God has done is to follow Joshua's example. We read in the Old Testament that Joshua built an altar of stones to commemorate what God had done in his life. Allow your congregation to do this too. Give everyone a rock, stone, or block of wood. Invite them to write one word about what God has done in their lives. Then either build your own altar on campus, or allow people to take the mementos home with them.

Whatever way you choose to honor God, be sure to incorporate these simple musts:

- Encourage small groups to enter the weekend service in clusters and sit together.

- Make it as experiential as possible. Provide a microphone for people to stand up and share testimonies. Invite a group on stage to share what God did and what's next for them. This is a great time to capture stories.

- Share praises, progress, and plans. We'll be sending you a census this week. Be sure to send it out to your leadership teams and small groups so they can complete it and let you know how to move forward.

B. ENCOURAGE MULTIPLE CELEBRATIONS.

Many churches just do a weekend celebration. It's more beneficial, however, to do three separate celebrations. **Start with a leadership celebration, then move to a weekend celebration, and finish with a small group celebration.** Here's what you need to know for each.

Leadership celebration — Do this during Weeks 4, 5, or Week 6 at the latest. Make it a really special event to ensure 100 percent participation. Hold it on a weekend and send out nice invitations. Invite the core people who helped with the campaign. Follow up the invitations with an e-mail reminder for responses or regrets. Then call anyone who doesn't respond to the e-mail.

Make sure the senior pastor attends the event. This will communicate importance to the leaders. Ask leaders to share one wild thing that happened, one wonderful thing, and what is next for their groups. Be sure to capture these stories in writing. Also, incorporate a memorable worship experience. You could include music, a foot washing ceremony, or even a candlelit communion service.

Before guests leave the event, get confirmation from them. Share praises, problems, and plans. Find out what they are going to do next. Ask them to give you feedback on who they think is the next wave of leaders.

Weekend celebration — Do this after you've held the leadership celebration. Don't only celebrate what God has done, but what he will continue to do. Cast a vision for the next step. Show previews or clips from the next curriculum series. You've already asked your congregation and small group members for six weeks, so now ask them to keep going.

Small group celebration — At the leadership and weekend celebrations, challenge small groups to hold their own celebration event during Week 7. Provide a care package for each small group filled with the next curriculum's DVD and book, a survey, and an agenda. Host the event away from your church campus and do activities that affirm, encourage, and inspire group members. Bathe the event in prayer.

C. ASK THEM TO CONTINUE THE JOURNEY.

If you don't do this, you will lose at least 50 percent of your groups. You must remember that the 40 Day campaign is casting a vision to cultivate five biblical purposes for life. **The campaign is not the destination; it is part of the journey.**

You can continue the journey by offering one of several curriculum series. One is the *Doing Life Together* study. This study provides a 30-week pilgrimage through the five biblical purposes, spending six weeks on each purpose. You could also lead *Experiencing Christ Together*. This is a six-session study that looks at the key character traits taught and modeled by Jesus that are essential to a life of service. Other options for continuing the journey include a Bible study series like James or 1 Thessalonians. It's a natural progression then to move into the Sermon on the Mount series in the fall.

Look at the long-term goals, not the immediate future. Your small group members are so teachable right now. Rather than letting them aimlessly wander to any other curriculum, keep them in the five purposes you worked so hard to launch. **You want to move them from having a taste of the purposes to being transformed by the purposes.** Cast a vision for a one-year pathway where they can develop the purposes in their own lives.

D. REGROUP AND RECOMMEND A NEXT STEP.

Use this opportunity to rotate leadership and host homes so no one gets burned out. This will help sustain your small groups since **25 percent of groups that disband do so because they didn't rotate.** If someone doesn't want to stay in a group, try holding a community connection event. This type of event allows people to get together in groups of two to four based on where they live. Encourage groups to share their spiritual journeys, their small group experience, and where they want to go. New small groups will launch as a result.

In addition to regrouping, it's important to recommend a next step. Suggesting a six-week series will help groups not lose momentum over the holidays. They can do the first three weeks before Christmas, and then complete the study in January.

Whatever curriculum you choose, be sure you clearly state what's next. If not, you'll lose some of your groups.

At the end of the celebration event or service, provide a registration form so people can pre-order or a sheet where they can sign up. Also be sure to have 30 to 50 percent of the next curriculum available. You may also consider purchasing a starter kit, which is one book and one DVD, of the curriculum of your choice as a gift for each small group.

E. TRAIN LEADERS FOR LIFE.

There are numerous ways to train your leaders to be lifelong pioneers. Here are a few great resources:

40 Day campaign small group champion and small group leader/member <u>newsletter series.</u> You'll receive the latest in small group ministry news and resources, and also participate with us as we interact with you through the polls and on our <u>Community</u> section.

Small Group University. Get your new leaders Hosting Lifetogether and your existing leaders Coaching Lifetogether to further train them.

The goal of the 40 Day campaign is to catalyze your small group ministry to be five to 10 times what you currently have. One of the most critical — and enjoyable — ways to do that is through celebration. Get to the **heart** of the matter and don't underestimate the power a little celebrating can have in your church.

TOP SEVEN LIST FOR THE "NOW WHAT" MOMENT

1. **Reload and Re-fire** - The number one mistake several of my closest pastor friends have made is to get enamored with the small group harvest and then let every one settle back into those cozy couches and chairs. Now they are like traditional small groups that exist primarily for the purpose of fellowship and Bible study (discipleship). Instead expect every existing group to not just do life together but to give life. The two best ways to do this are to constantly rotate leadership and to develop in any church, an unlimited army of leaders over time.

2. **Focus on What Really Matters** - my basic of all basics is to stay spiritually healthy, support your existing leaders with a fairly flat structure leveraging email and infrequent rallies and most importantly senior pastors are the number one growth engine of any church. Your job is to somehow convince them (Sr. Pastors) of their need and give them the opportunity to do so. This is a near to impossible, frustrating, humiliating, job threatening affair. Trust me I know your pain! With out mentioning who or where I was really hurt several times but I pressed on. Needless to say, today I have unlimited job security and don't get called "Johnny one note" any more. Do you know why? Because I listened (most of the time) and worked hard at serving who ever God put into that role. Let my scars speak to you and you will enjoy a greater harvest.

3. **Curriculum is the second most important tool** - Many churches I have consulted with did what I call old country western style "40 Days of Purpose Campaigns". Launch them, Love them and leave them…way before they were ready. Groups that have a continued DVD/video driven launch need a similar resource in the next few series they do. What is the use of starting these groups if you also need to sustain them? Ideally a Five Purpose Series with a Master Teacher and a training segment is best. This builds more grace than pastors have any idea. Actually, it changes the entire DNA of what is needed before during and after. We have actually called the new Doing Lifetogether™ curriculum, *"One Year of Purpose Together"*. It's a follow up series and it takes the taste of the purposes to a point of transforming people's lives through the purposes.

4. **Embrace that a greater reformation is yet to come** - Most churches and their pastors and their members had no idea what was coming. Church life will from this day

forward never be the same. One person asked a Saddleback Staff member, "Have we become a cell or home church?' Another said, "What impact will this have on our midweek services?" Another said, "What would happen if we had a Sunday School program?" Please even as you read this don't close your fist, but open your palms if you can because greater implications are in the works…for example, when we had more people in one week… 2500…that wanted to get into groups than was regularly attending midweek and we had 4000 others in midweek groups we decide to end a 15 year Saddleback tradition. Churches all around the country will struggle with this question, especially when they get into the second and third phase of their small group efforts. Evangelizing resources, infrastructure will be reallocated, budgets will be shifted, building designs will change and every body will need to buy a video camera. The sooner you see it the sooner you can help others process it.

5. **Focus on what really matters.** - Recruiting new hosts is 10x's more vital that connecting members. It's the difference from spiritual addition and multiplication. Get on the bus or get off because you will be left behind. The real question is do you want to commit 100% of your congregation or 50-70%? You can get 125% +. Leadership rallies, end of year small group staff lunches, celebrations, retreats all catalyze leadership community events that help build community and culture. Best of all it gives you one of 100 reasons to get your senior staff in the game.

6. **Begin with the end in mind.** - The end is to build healthy, balanced churches, groups, and lives. Whatever it takes to first get them in is key. Then turn the crock pot of the group temperature way up. Use a survey to have them self assess their own health. And do it with the entire church as well. (Download a free assessment on our site). Also remember connecting people is only the first step…cultivating health is the ultimate goal. That's why again, a balance of the curriculum, preaching on the weekend, weekly group agenda and seasonal group alignment is critical. Bill Hybels once said its not the seekers that need the weekend but the believers. We all need to be reminded of what on earth we are here for. As Rick Warren said in the first line of his book – It's not about you – and when it comes to your group its not about them either but God and God alone.

7. **Recruit and develop a senior leader of leaders** - Return to a bi-vocational model of Staff -Why to get the "best" leaders on this clock. Many times. the typical staff drawn to small group ministry have gifts of shepherding, and encouragement but not leadership and administration. They are care givers not campaign managers, challengers of next and certainly not leaders of leaders of leaders. I know this one is a bit scary but it's just the truth. Three of the small group pastors in the 40 Day churches have been let go. Why? Not good people? Not capable? No, they just didn't have the big "L" Leadership gifts. They may not be on your staff or your current team but they are in your church. Ask for the senior pastor's help to recruit the best set of gifts your church needs. I have had two people in my life promoted over me. 1st was hard 2nd I was ready to hand it over – you know even now what is needed. Trust your leading before God and He will lead you.

COMMITTED TO COMMUNITY
WHY CHURCHES EVERYWHERE ARE DISCOVERING THE DIFFERENCE RELATIONAL MINISTRY CAN MAKE

It seems like small groups are popping up everywhere. And churches that have a recognized small group ministry are becoming more the standard than the exception. Why is that? What's going on?

As director of smallgroups.com, I had a lot of contact with churches that were neck deep in the small group movement. My job revolved around helping pastors and small group leaders keep their small groups active and healthy. So I got a lot of feedback about what's driving the rise of small group ministry.

There are definitely many dynamics involved in the small group movement, but I've noticed a common thread. And that is the strong desire people have to experience genuine community. People are seeing the need for a kind of community that's really missing in our information age culture. There are a lot of broken lives and a lot of dysfunction in traditional relationships and the family so the whole idea of bringing a New Testament community back into the church is something people see and feel they need.

I witnessed this phenomenon first hand in my own church. As the church grew to a point where it was impossible to know everyone, people began to feel disconnected. That's when someone suggested we give small groups a try. Many responded with great enthusiasm. It wasn't difficult to get people involved, but after a while, the "honeymoon phase" wore off. Once the congregation got into community with each other, they began to realize, "I liked you better when I didn't know you as well." But just as in marriage, many soon realized they needed to be committed to the building of community whether they always liked it or not.

The interesting thing that happened through it all was that in the process of getting people into small groups, a value was raised up. People began to realize that relational ministry makes a difference. And that kind of ministry is more than just showing up on Sunday morning or doing nursery duty.

My church's experience is definitely not unique. It's a common story I hear. As churches venture into small group ministry, they uncover the richness of and the great need for genuine relationships. What's more, many people begin to view their small community as the heart and essence of what they feel church is like for them. I think that's because many small groups are incorporating a lot of elements of what the New Testament describes as church, especially in the area of relationships with one another.

Building true community isn't always an easy process. I learned that with my church family. But I believe it's what followers of Christ are called to do—to live life together. That's the model of the New Testament. And even if it is difficult, following Christ is the most incredible thing we can do in life. But the deeper we get into it, the more we have to rely on Him to do it.

LEADERSHIP CELEBRATION:

Holding a celebration for your small group hosts/leaders is a great way to honor and celebrate your small group hosts/leaders. It celebrates that step of faith they took to host a group as they invited others to join them. It also celebrates what God is doing in the hearts and lives of the individuals in each of their groups. It expands the vision and gives people an opportunity to share in the larger community of faith.

It also motivates your hosts and their groups to continue after the 40 Day campaign.

In preparation for the celebration you will need to decide on the next curriculum so you are ready to have the next series in the hands of the hosts by campaign Week 4 or 5. For September campaign churches, that is the beginning of October, and for October campaign churches that is at the end of October. If you decide now and get a sample order in right away it will make a 30-50 percent difference in the number of groups that continue. If you wait until the end of the campaign to communicate what's next or wait to continue until after the first of the year, you will have lost momentum and have to do a complete restart of a cold engine. We discussed what to order last week. We encourage you to select one of the purpose studies specifically either "Service" or "Worship." You can also do the *Inside Out Living* study by Lance Witt.

Well there is no better communication than face-to-face communication. We encourage you to gather your hosts/leaders together in Week 4 of the campaign to celebrate what God has done together by sharing stories and instructing them in the purposes. If you have a large church we encourage your coaches or community leaders to do it in their homes. If you have a smaller church, we encourage you to gather everyone together to hear what God is doing across your church. If you can do it in your home it is better, but doing it at the church works as well. Encourage each host/leader to invite someone else from the group to come with them to catch the vision.

Your goal is 100 percent participation in it. Aim as high as you can. Make it a nice wedding invitation and mail it to them. Then follow up by phone to get their RSVP. Tell them in the invitation it will be a blast and lots of fun together. You can ask them one wild thing and something wonderful and what is next. Capture stories by having them write it out in a paragraph as them come to the event.

Here is an outline for what you can do during the host/leader celebration:

Leadership event outline:

Make this a real time of acknowledgement and appreciation. Use candles and table cloths or supply the food for a barbeque either go to a special place or have it catered. People want to hear what else is happening out there. The event is like a family reunion where we bring them back together for stories, news, updates, prayer, love, fellowship, and just to celebrate what we've done as we've separated from each other.

To do this, have them gather in tables. Designate a table leader. Provide food for them and encourage the table leader to get the discussion going while they are eating. Place 3x5 cards on the table and have them answer a couple of questions in preparation for their discussion:

What is one praise – a story or something that is working well?

- What is one problem – a leadership challenge or something that is not working?
- Open with prayer and encourage them to eat and have discussion about stories at their tables.
- Transition to a large group experience.
- Spend some time in worship together. Use one of the worship DVD's to model what they can do in their small group.
- Have the senior pastor stop in and share appreciation for what they have done, reflect on what God is doing in our midst and where we are going as a result of it.
- Take time to share testimonies from reluctant hosts/coaches and hear what God did through their reluctance.
- Share testimonies of what God is doing inside the groups. Request these stories before the event.
- Reinforce principles from the host briefing about the purposes and share stories of how the groups are beginning to practice them in their groups.
- Use a slide show or video of various groups especially doing community service projects or meeting together.
- Share with them what you would like the groups to do next. Provide a sample curriculum at each table and ask the table leaders to ask the question: What do you think your group would like to do next? Give them a card to fill out to let you know so you can support them. If they can't fill it out right then ask them to complete it and get it back to you by the Week 5 or 6.
- Either provide the curriculum at the event for them to purchase or have fliers available for them to know how they can get the material either by ordering through you or directly on the Web site, www.lifetogether.com.
- End with praying together in groups of three or four people across the room and finish with a worship song with everyone.

This event is a great opportunity to celebrate what God is doing and cast vision and ask for commitment for the groups to continue.

BUILDING LIFETOGETHER APPENDIX

BUILDING LIFETOGETHER ANSWER KEY

Session 1:
Connecting
Cultivate
Create
Coaching
Creating

Session 2:
Biblical
Reproducible
Relational
Beneficial
Experimental
Developmental
Transferable
Systems
Spiritual
Seasonal

Session 3:
Call
Challenge
Communicate
Curriculum
Campaigns
Constituents
- Core
- Committed
- Crowd

Senior Pastor
Small Group Champion/Pastor
Coach

Session 4:
Begin
Create
Curriculum
Launch 'em
Align
New Host
Focus
Select
Measure
Secret

Session 5:
Grow
Qualifications
Minister
Mentor
Motivate
Multiply
Model
Build
- Loyal
- Leadership
- Love
- Lives
- Let
- Like

Session 6:
Devine
Redefine
Create
Rally
Plan
Leverage
Model
Catalyze
Create
Come

PASTOR FAQ'S

Here are common questions from Pastor's.

How do I launch a small group ministry?
The key is vision casting... almost every church wants to grow in numbers and reach out to their community. Vision casting is explaining the dream of Jesus Christ, "that every sheep would have a shepherd," meaning that every believer would be connected to one another so that the body of Christ could fulfill its purpose. It's also giving your church body easy tools through which they can accomplish this purpose. A small group ministry and a church campaign can do all of this at once and has some amazing fringe benefits like growth in church attendance and giving as well as building an effective engine through which the senior pastor and staff can communicate to their church body. These fringe benefits help the reluctant Pastors and staff and leadership to see the value and purpose of being a church of small groups not a church with small groups. Begin with setting the vision then implement a plan to recruit small group hosts and small group members.

How do I launch a small group ministry in a traditional or Sunday School church?
Either start carefully and small, or do a church-wide launch, like when you do a capital campaign. "All hands on deck", from preschool to adults and all ministries included, have them all be part of a spiritual growth campaign for the whole church. For a smaller version, try a few bible study classes and start by using round tables to sit at. This will divide the people up, then have one person at each table facilitate the questions (not a table leader, do this softly) and have all the classes study the same curriculum together... they will naturally or organically become a small group just by sharing answers to the curriculum questions in a smaller more intimate circle.

When do I start small groups or a small group ministry?
NOW! The #1 need among people is to belong... to be in relationship with other people. If this is true, then small groups are the answer to this need in the context of churches as well as outside of the church. We have found that the very best time of year to start small groups is in the fall when school has started back up and summer vacations are over. Then follow the seasons, with January and Easter as two other prime launch times for small groups. January is a good restart time, when people are open to new ideas and programs and after Easter is prime time for new believer and new attendee/ member groups to begin.

How do I effectively assimilate church attendees into groups?
Probably the most important factor here is to communicate the vision from the pulpit through testimonies and stories of what and how small groups are doing in people's lives. The stories of life transforming life in the individual members of your congregation will have greater impact than any ask you can do. The Senior Pastor's own buy in, and listing the benefits of being in a small group are also key motivating factors. When the Senior Pastors says I am going to a group too" the ripple effect is contagious, everyone wants to "belong" ... so jump on that band wagon and use it to draw people in.

Where do I find leaders?
Most groups have a host or hostess. A Host is simply; someone who has a HEART for people, is willing to OPEN heir home, will SERVE a pot of coffee and TURN on the VCR or DVD for the teaching part of the study. It's so easy that way; you are simply a facilitator for the evening and could easily rotate this task among the group each week. We encourage you to select one or more discussion leaders and one or more host /leaders /facilitators for each group. We recommend that you rotate the job of facilitating your discussions, hosting the study at their house etc. thus creating opportunities for everyone's gifts to develop. Several other responsibilities can be rotated, including refreshments, prayer requests, worship, or keeping up with those who miss a meeting. Shared ownership in the group helps everybody grow and feel a commitment to the group.

How do I inspire and motivate people to get involved?
Your main objective will be to spark a vision within the hearts of your lay leaders, as their roles will be primary in this small group movement. I think there are three leadership principles that will help you do this successfully.

BUILDINGLIFE**TOGETHER**

Lead with your heart. You've heard it time and again. People need to know that you care before they care what you know. They need to see your heart for them. So when it comes to equipping your small group leaders, the best thing you can do is to follow the example of Jesus, who called his disciples to be with him. This means not only doing ministry together but doing Lifetogether. Invite them to dinner. Find out about their lives. Then you will be better able to love them, cheer them on, and show gratitude for them.

Love them with your hands. Those who are involved in leading small groups are going to need a lot of encouragement. A handshake from you, a high five, or a note of affirmation can work wonders in a weary heart. When you follow up with them and let them know they are doing a good job, you potentially provide fuel to keep them focused and motivated. Another way to keep them going is to remind them of the big picture, how small groups are a means to grow believers and build up the church.

Listen with your head. When you meet with small group leaders, you should be prepared with thoughtful questions and challenges. Then as you listen to their responses, you can encourage them to launch what they are suggesting, to take ownership of their ideas. People love following a leader, but people follow those who let them lead.

And by the way, I wouldn't worry too much about whether or not your congregation will get involved. Even though everyone is so busy, the desire to belong is greater than their busy feeling. In fact, this need for belonging is the strongest felt need in society. So be encouraged that you're on the right track toward meeting people where they are.

SMALL GROUP CHAMPION FAQ'S

Here are common questions from Small Group Ministry Leaders.

Why do you recommend recruiting "hosts?" What is a "Host Home" concept?
Most churches, even with a decent small group ministry, need to launch new groups with new leaders. And if you have no small group ministry—it's the only way to begin.

So, what is the bottleneck of small groups in most churches?
Leaders. If you could crack the code for recruiting and developing leaders, your ministry would explode. We've found the best way for that to happen is to launch a 6-week small group campaign in your church. It has a beginning and an end—and so people feel it's doable. And you don't ask for leaders. You publicly invite people to open their homes to host one of these groups. People are not intimidated by opening up their home. We've found that when churches ask for hosts—they blow the doors off—they end up with more hosts than they expected. And then they struggle to fill each Host Home with 8 to 12 members. It's a wonderful problem to have—more hosts than people to fill the home.

So, a Host is simply someone or a couple who opens their home for a six-week study. And then, in the coaching process, we help churches identify the leaders in each group. The purpose of a "Designed for Life" group, for example, is to engage—in the context of community—to answer the question: "What is God's design for my life?" We encourage churches to align their weekend services with the six-week campaign. It simultaneously combines the weekend services and the formation of people in small groups on the same topic: to focus on and practice God's core values in our lives—together.

How do I recruit and train new leaders/hosts?
First, stop recruiting "leaders" and start recruiting people who would be willing to open their home! With the Video and DVD curriculums available from Lifetogether or others, ordinary members can lead or "host" a group like never before. Your response will be 10:1 of previous methods. We used to say, "If you can read, you can lead". Now, we say, "If you have a DVD, just watch it and see.".

Second, rotate the leadership of your groups weekly. This is the most natural way to cultivate an unlimited harvest of leaders for any group. One group, one leader at a time—what I call the "crock pot method" of leadership development. This has become the most revolutionary approach to preparing the soil for an upcoming harvest.

Finally, recognize that ultimately, it is not about your great training program; it's more about getting people into groups and just watching what God does through the lives of ordinary leaders and their groups. The Bible says that Paul planted, Apollo watered but God caused the growth. Simply pray to the Lord of the harvest, get them into community, and watch God do the rest.

What is a Host responsible for?
Opening their home to a few friends and church family, plugging in the DVD, and facilitating a few questions for six weeks using the bible study curriculum you've selected. Hosts may also encourage personal reading time by all the group members using a devotional book or journal.

If I am a Host, for example, who ends up being in the six-week study?
Your small group consists of between 8 and 12 members. You are able to choose how your group gets formed—you can have people assigned to your group and/or invited by you! Here are what your options look like:

A. Friends of the Host: You may fill your group with people you know from your church or with your spiritually seeking friends who do not attend.
B. Friends of the Church: Your small group ministry team or person will automatically assign church people who sign up for your time and type of group unless you inform the team that your group is filled with those you have personally invited.
C. Friends of friends: Friends of Friends are another primary way a Host may fill their groups. One couple knows another couple and they know about ten other people, the rest is history.

Should Hosts invite people only from the church or seeker friends?

That is totally up to the Host. The point is to seek God prayerfully about who to invite. Hundreds of new groups have welcomed their unbelieving neighbors and seeking friends.

What happens at the end of the six-week starter groups?
In the 4th week of your study, we recommend that the Hosts invite the members of their group to continue for another six-week study. Some groups will continue, some will join other groups & some members and/or groups will stop meeting. Make sure you have a curriculum plan for the entire year. You'll be surprised how many groups will continue.

What about Hosts that don't want to continue after the first six-week study?
We ask the Hosts, then, in this instance, to prayerfully ask God to make apparent someone among the group who can replace him or her. That is the hope—an ongoing, life-giving, healthy small group. Someone needs to be identified as the "point person" for the group, but responsibilities can be rotated, including refreshments, prayer requests, worship and keeping up with those who miss a meeting. Shared ownership in the group helps everyone grow.

How do I equip and develop leaders?
We have found that 90% of equipping and development of leaders can be done through what we call "just in time training" within the curriculum we have produced. A large part of developing leaders is based on relationships but ease of facilitating a small group takes away all fears. Regular meetings at your church after the initial 6 weeks will keep the hosts informed and educated.

How do I "pre-engineer" for major growth in the number of groups?
One of the best ways we have found to deal with large growth is to identify the groups by geography first and then if needed by affinity (couples, singles, women and men groups). Once you have assessed this assign staff or lay leadership (which we call division leaders/community leaders) over 20-25 groups preferably in their neighborhood area. Not only does this give these "Coaches/supervisors value but proximity that helps the "ownership" factor to be high, if the groups are in their area and in their affinity/ life stage.

How do you re-engineer existing small groups?
One of the easiest ways is to conduct a whole church spiritual growth campaign and have every ministry and age level, studying the same thing. If everyone is included in the vision and the plan for growth, 85% of the existing groups will buy into the program. At several churches the Senior Pastors have also asked all ministries and groups to NOT MEET for a period of 6-8 weeks (depending on the curriculum) so that every one of the members can go out and host or co-host a group for the growth campaign. It's also important to have a curriculum that prioritizes the importance of rotating leadership. This accomplishes the re-engineering without the "birthing" pain; they don't even know they are changing.

Wondering what to do on Day 41 of the campaign?
The Doing Lifetogether Series has become one of the best follow-up curriculums to the 40 Days of Purpose campaign. This Purpose Driven™ Group Resource has been recommended by Rick Warren as the first series built completely on the Purpose Driven™ paradigm. If you finished the campaign last fall or this spring you can recommend to your small groups and Sunday School classes to begin right away. All you need is a six week window and your groups can test drive the next six week series in this exciting new study on the purposes. It follows the same format of the 40 Days of Purpose and allows for a more complete study on each purpose. We recommend you study either the "Connecting with God's Family" (fellowship study) first, then the "Grow to be more like Christ" (discipleship study). Don't worry if you can't complete all six sessions before the Thanksgiving and Christmas break; this will help to ensure the group sticks together over the holidays. The final recommendation is to use the "Sharing your Life Mission Everyday" (Evangelism study) immediately following the Grow study and marching up to the cross together as a group or church at Easter. One church improved their Easter attendance by almost 40% by having all their groups go through the study at the same time. Lifetogether also has other studies available, visit our website for our latest offerings.

How do you make groups become really meaningful for participants?
Feed their need... A group can be meaningful to it's participants for many reasons, from relationships to physical, mental, and emotional needs being met, to accomplishing a goal together, to serving a greater good together... the essence is in 'doing Lifetogether." God created us to be in relationship with Him first and then each other not far behind. Figure out what your groups want by listening... and you will not be disappointed by the results of ... Feeding their need.

What curriculum should I use?
There are many good choices of bible study curriculum for small groups. Lifetogether has a wonderful series we recommend you consider because of its purpose based philosophy and its DVD components. Go to lifetogether.com for more information.

THE LIFETOGETHER PATHWAY

The Lifetogether Pathway outlines a simple road map through one year of a small group or entire church going through the purposes. Whether this is your first experience to the 5-purpose model or you've just completed a 40 Day Campaign, the Lifetogether Pathway can guide you each step of the way.

The "One Year of Ministry Plan"

TARGET AUDIENCE	JAN/FEB	APRIL/MAY	SEPT/OCT	NOV/DEC
	6 Weeks	6 Weeks	6 Weeks	6 Weeks
Purpose	Fellowship/Evangelism	Ministry/Fellowship	Discipleship/Fellowship	Worship/5 Purposes
DLT Adults	*Connect or Grow then Share	Develop (Existing Group Connect (New Groups)	*Grow or Connect/Begin	Surrender (into the holidays)
DLT Students	Connect / Share	Serve	Grow/Start	Honor
Lifetogether Worship Series	Connect / Grow	Connect / Grow	Begin	Surrender
Lifetogether Training Series (Small Group Leadership)	Launching	Coaching	Leading & Coaching	Coaching & Leading

* Service and Small Group Alignment

BUILDING LIFE TOGETHER

Beginning Lifetogether (Overview of the Purposes) - Provides an opening lesson of the Great Commandment and the Great Commission that explains the essence or Goal of Life. Then the following five weeks gives you a one-week session on each purpose. This is an excellent book to introduce your existing groups to the series or to launch your entire church into small groups. It's an excellent starter curriculum and is similar to the 40 Days of Purpose curriculum from Saddleback Church. We recommend launching with the 40 Days of Purpose material and then using the Doing Lifetogether series as a follow-up to the campaign. This is best to use as a kickoff for the fall, New Year or post Easter. There is a parallel student edition to this series by Doug Fields the author of the Purpose Driven™ Youth Ministry.

Connecting with God's Family (Fellowship) - This is a highly relational study and is an excellent follow up to the Beginning Lifetogether Study or the 40 Days of Purpose campaign. It is also a great way to kick off your first groups in the fall or even in the New Year. The felt need of relationships, belonging and community are naturally very high. Several groups and churches have been very successful in launching groups after Easter or even multiplying their existing groups using this highly relational series. There are some very popular and welcoming teachers on this particular series.

Growing to be Like Christ (Discipleship) - This is one of the strongest studies in the whole series. It is an excellent choice for groups turning the New Year or for after Easter as well as starting off in the fall. It's a parallel study to some of the Navigator-like studies that challenge a deeper walk and Henry Blackaby's Experiencing God material. The response to this series is very high.

Developing your Shape for Ministry - This series is like having a gift discovery class (i.e. Network or Class 301) in a small group setting. Taught by people like Erwin Mc Manus, Carol Kent, and Bruce Wilkinson, this series has your group not just discovering their gifts but doing something with their gifts. The practical "baby steps" in this series has 90% of the group serving in some roles as a team together. No one likes serving alone. The group serves together in community. Finally, by the end of the six weeks every member has discovered their unique God given SHAPE for ministry, and the group has helped them develop their gifts somewhere in the church and/or community. Most pastors and church leaders love that this study produces mobilization, not just information. And members love this study because it's always fun learning how God uniquely made us - especially when the affirmation flows.

Sharing Your Life Mission Everyday (Evangelism) – This series is primarily for believers. It is a good time to motivate believers to get connected and prepare for the church to open up their arms, homes and the doors to the weekend services. This six-week series is like a small group version of Evangelism Explosion, Contagious Christian, or other popular or trench evangelism training programs.

The most powerful time for this series is the 6-8 weeks before Easter or in the fall leading up to Christmas. It helps when the pastor teaches parallel passages on the weekend. It helps people to reach out to unchurched and uncommitted people and then the study trains them on how to do it. One church increased their weekend attendance by 40% at Easter by simply having their congregation go through the series together as a church in their groups and Sunday School. We recommend this series be followed with a study like "Connect", "Grow", or "Beginning Lifetogether".

Surrendering Your Heart for Worship – This series is the most passionate series of them all. Some churches are using this book first after the 40 Days of Purpose in the fall or spring because it follows the natural order of Rick Warren's book, The Purpose Driven Life™. Surrendering your heart for God's Pleasure is a great option for those heading into the holidays and especially those preparing to roll out a capital campaign.

ONE YEAR OF PURPOSE GOALS

	TOTAL NUMBER	CURRENT # GROUPS	YEAR_____ EXPONENTIAL GOAL
# Calling our church their church home			
Avg. Adult Worship Attendance			
# Children's Ministry			
# in on Campus Adult Classes			
# in Off Campus Groups			
# in Men's Ministry			
# in Women's Ministry			
# in Single's Ministy			
# in H.S. & J.H. Ministry			
# in College Ministry			
TOTAL GROUPS			

HOST ORIENTATION AGENDA

The purpose of the Host Orientation is to empower the hosts to have the best possible first experience. Build their confidence that they can do it well. They will be nervous if they are doing it for the first time and will want to know the best ways to make it a success. Your goal is to equip them by coaching them to:

1. **CREATE** their own community
   - ☐ Coach them on filling their group with the circles of life
   - ☐ Host a social and encourage all members to invite those in their circles of life
2. **CONNECT** their group
   - ☐ Make new members feel welcome
   - ☐ Propose a social event to help them grow in connecting in community.
3. **CULTIVATE** their Spiritual Journey
   - ☐ Share the health assessment with them
   - ☐ Encourage them to connect with their coach
4. **CHAMPION** their Gifts Together
   - ☐ Help them practice the purpose roles and rotate leadership
5. **COACH** Members to Shepherd Another
   - ☐ Encourage them to reach out and invite others
6. **CELEBRATE** Life Together
   - ☐ As a group and as a larger community

Key tips for you:
1. Ask Senior Pastor to attend for a few minutes and speak.
2. Distribute a Host pack to all hosts containing:
   a. Cover Letter from Senior Pastor
   b. DVD
   c. 8 books
   d. Invitation Scripts
   e. Roster of unconnected people
   f. Collection/Roster Envelope
   g. 30 post cards or business cards
   h. Host frequently asked questions
   i. Story Pages
3. Ask the Community Leaders / Coaches to invite their hosts and sit with them when possible.
4. Hold at least 2 orientations, one on the weekend and one during the week. The numbers of orientations are dependent on the space available and the number of hosts. We have found that you will get a high attendance for this orientation because, for many, it's the first time they have hosted a group. They want to be successful.
5. During Host orientation, show the Hosts how to access the just in time training on the DVD and the training resources in the back of the study guide. Then toward the end of the campaign before the next series ask the community leaders to help gather Hosts in their homes to view the leading life together material together and discuss it.

CONNECTING ANNOUNCEMENT SCRIPT

All across America people are gathering in homes to worship and pray together, study God's word, discover the gifts God has given them, fellowship and practice the one another's from the bible, and share God's love with those in their community and ultimately go into the uttermost parts of the earth. All this is being done in Small Groups.

This fall, we are launching a community based initiative called *40 Days of Purpose*. It will run for six weeks starting in September. Our desire is to give everyone associated with (Our Church) the opportunity to do what the early church did: Temple Courts and House to House.

Do you own or rent a home? Do you have a TV and VCR? Do you know how to operate your TV and VCR? (Always an important question to ask!) Do you know how to pop a bag of popcorn? Could you brew a pot of coffee? Or if you rather, could you open up a bag of Cheetoes and pour a 2-liter bottle of Pepsi? Do you think you might be able to tell a couple of friends about it?

If say yes to those things you can H.O.S.T. a group. Would you be willing to H.O.S.T. a group in your home so that others can receive that gift of community?

Mathew 9:36 says that when Jesus saw the crowds, he had compassion on them, because they were harassed and helpless, like sheep without a shepherd. When I look across the crowds who come to First Assembly Ministries to worship, I see the faces of many connected and many unconnected people. There are people in our church and in our community who because they are unconnected have not experienced what the early church experienced soon after the day of Pentecost, people to love them and care for one another. Would you be willing to take a step of faith and help connect the unconnected?

H.O.S.T. (on a power point screen)

H eart for people

O pen your home

S erve a few snacks

T ell a few friends

If you have a **Heart** for people, are willing to **Open** your home, **Serve** a few Snacks and **Tell** a few friends, family, neighbors, co-workers and others to join you for 6 weeks to watch a DVD of nationally known teachers like we just saw, you can H.O.S.T. a group. If you could pick any group of people to hang out with for the next 6 weeks who would you choose? Family members, friends, relatives. Who do you really like to hang out with? That's who you can invite.

94 BUILDINGLIFETOGETHER

Some of you are long time attenders of (Our Church). Some of you are coming for the first time today. This opportunity is for everyone.

We want everyone to join us as we go on this new adventure this fall. Sign-up today by filling out the insert in your bulletin and dropping it in the offering basket then attending the first Host Orientation this Thursday, August 25th at _____ home at _____ PM. (*put date time and place on the second power point screen*) Thanks, you'll be glad you did.

SMALL GROUP COACH MINISTRY DESCRIPTION

The purpose of the Host Training to prepare the hosts to shepherd their members. Your role as a coach is to:

1. **MINISTER TO THE NEEDS OF YOUR LEADERS _AND_ THEIR MEMBERS**
    - In a healthy small group, the members as well as the leaders must be "healthy".
    - You define success by the health of your small group members.
    - Leaders need to love on and pray for each member.
    - It's VIP to do this in the first few weeks to establish this biblical purpose of "fellowship".

2. **MENTOR THEIR SPIRITUAL MATURITY TO GROW TO BE LIKE CHRIST**
    - Help to cultivate their spiritual habits (in devotion, worship, finance, stewardship, family, etc).
    - How? You must know the condition of your sheep. What is the next step in their spiritual maturity? Help to cultivate this.

3. **MOTIVATE THEIR "SHAPE" (SPIRITUAL GIFTS) FOR MINISTRY**
    - Modeling it in your own life will result in the "trickle down" effect.
    - Do your sheep know your gifts? Are they growing in their gifts?
    - Where are they serving now?

4. **MULTIPLY THEIR LIFE & MISSION**
    - Multiply your life into the life of another.
    - Multiply your group.
    - Give away the life you've been given.

5. **MODEL A SURRENDERED HEART**
    - Allow yourself to be transparent in front of your group.
    - Never forget that this is a work of God Almighty.
    - If you're making a difference in other people's lives expect spiritual warfare
    - God works best in our weakness…that's when HE IS STRONG.
    - What is your Isaac? What do you need to lay down on the altar to be consumed by the fire of His presence?
    - God loves to hear the confessions and prayers of a broken and contrite heart.
    - Worship HIM no matter what the circumstances with a thankful and hopeful heart.

Key tips for you:
1. The video training is intended to be decentralized. Hold the training either in one 2.5 hour session or in two 1.5 hour sessions over two weeks.
2. The video training is intended to be interactive. It's best to have groups of no more than five discussing the questions together in order to get the most participation.
3. We recommend holding the training after the first 6 weeks of hosting a group.

ROLE OF COMMUNITY LEADER

Purpose:

To fulfill the mission of the church by managing, ministering, and administering the spiritual development of individuals by ensuring the growth and expansion of 20 or more small groups.

Requirement:

Be able to volunteer five to 15 hours per week for thee to four months during mid-August through November to fulfill this ministry as a staff member of the church.

Qualifications:

- Loyalty to the senior pastor and the senior leaders of the church
- A proven gift of leadership inside and outside of the church
- Committed to the principle of doing life together (demonstrated by the personal life style of living life together in the church)
- Life reflecting the character of a deacon – 1 Timothy 3:8-13
- A growing walk with Christ

Expectations:

Community leaders will assist with the management of the small group ministry by assuming managerial responsibilities for 15-25 H.O.S.T.s and their small group members.

The community leader will:

- Gather H.O.S.T.s as needed for meetings, rally's, and retreats.
- Assess the needs of every H.O.S.T.
- Find a shepherd for every H.O.S.T. based on the individual needs of the H.O.S.T.
- Ensure communication with the assigned H.O.S.T.s occurs to make sure they have what they need in providing guidance in filling groups, facilitation skills, focusing on the five purposes, etc.
- Assist in the "transitions" of each group to the follow up study or whatever is next for the group.

The vision is that each H.O.S.T. will have someone that will minister, mentor, motivate and assist in the multiplication of each group. The community leader is responsible for that to happen.

Primary responsibilities:
- Pray for the coaches and H.O.S.T. s under your care during the campaign.
- Gather the H.O.S.T.s together in the beginning of the campaign to meet them and encourage them.
- Provide training and/or follow-up with the H.O.S.T.s to make sure they have completed the training material given to the H.O.S.T. s.
- Provide H.O.S.T. s with a support structure (e.g. ask experienced H.O.S.T. s to help "coach" other H.O.S.T. s with you; or pair key H.O.S.T. s with less experienced H.O.S.T. s)
- Each community leader gathers their H.O.S.T. s together for mid-campaign encouragement and communication of the transition plan for new groups.
- Recruit and release new leaders from existing groups.

G.I.F.T.S. PROFILE WORKSHEET

To Help Discover Or Develop Your God-Given G.I.F.T.S.

Copy one to each member in your group. Have them fill out and then share with the group affirming or adding. Then assign base roles or empower ministry outside the group.

1) GIFTS (SPIRITUAL)
- ❏ Preaching (1 Cor. 14:3)
- ❏ Evangelism (Acts 8:26-40)
- ❏ Discernment (I John 4:1)
- ❏ Apostle (Rom. 15:20)
- ❏ Teaching (Eph. 4:12-13)
- ❏ Encouragement (Acts 14:22)
- ❏ Wisdom (I Cor. 2:1, 6-16)
- ❏ Missions (I Cor. 9:19-23, Acts 13:2-3)
- ❏ Service (Acts 6:1-7, I Cor. 12:28)
- ❏ Mercy (Romans 12:8)
- ❏ Hospitality (I Peter 4:9-10)
- ❏ Pastoring (I Peter 5:2-4)
- ❏ Giving (II Cor. 8:1-7)
- ❏ Intercession (Col. 1:9-12)
- ❏ Music (Psalm 150)
- ❏ Arts & Crafts (Exodus 31:3-11)
- ❏ Healing (James 5:14-16)
- ❏ Miracles (Mark 11:23-24)
- ❏ Leadership (Heb. 13:7, 17)
- ❏ Administration (I Cor. 14:40)
- ❏ Faith (Rom. 4:18-21)

2) INTERESTS & PASSIONS
- ❏ Design/Develop
- ❏ Pioneer
- ❏ Organize
- ❏ Operate/Maintain
- ❏ Serve/Help
- ❏ Acquire/Possess
- ❏ Excel
- ❏ Perform
- ❏ Improve
- ❏ Repair
- ❏ Lead/Be in Charge
- ❏ Persevere
- ❏ Follow the Rules
- ❏ Prevail
- ❏ Influence

3) FAMILIAR EXPERIENCES
- ❏ Spiritual
- ❏ Painful
- ❏ Educational
- ❏ Vocational
- ❏ Ministry

4) TEMPERAMENT

	HI	LOW	HI	
Extroverted	❏	❏	❏	Introverted
Routine	❏	❏	❏	Variety
Self-controlled	❏	❏	❏	Self-expressive
Cooperative	❏	❏	❏	Competitive

5) STRENGTHS
- ❏ Entertaining
- ❏ Recruiting
- ❏ Planning
- ❏ Evaluating
- ❏ Managing
- ❏ Researching
- ❏ Artistic/Graphics
- ❏ Interviewing
- ❏ Counseling
- ❏ Teaching
- ❏ Writing/Editing
- ❏ Promoting
- ❏ Repairing
- ❏ Feeding
- ❏ Recall
- ❏ Mechanical Operating
- ❏ Resourceful
- ❏ Counting/Classifying
- ❏ Public Relations
- ❏ Welcoming
- ❏ Composing
- ❏ Landscaping
- ❏ Arts & Crafts
- ❏ Decorating
- ❏ Musical

SMALL GROUP GIFT DEVELOPMENT TABLE

YOUR G.I.F.T.S.	WHAT DO YOU KNOW?	WHAT DO OTHERS SEE?	WHAT COULD BE NEXT?
Gifts (Spiritual)			
Interests & Passions			
Familiar Experiences			
Temperament (Personality)			
Strengths (Talents)			

PERSONAL HEALTH ASSESSMENT

CONNECTING with God's family

I am intentionally cultivating my relationships with Christian friends & spiritual mentors	1 2 3 4 5
I am cultivating authentic community by speaking truth in love and creating healthy boundaries	1 2 3 4 5
I am more loving, grace giving & forgiving to others than I was a year ago	1 2 3 4 5
I am resolving conflict with others in a Biblical manner, and supporting the leadership of this church family	1 2 3 4 5
I am willing to share my real needs for prayer and support with others	1 2 3 4 5

Connecting Total _____

GROWING to be like Christ

I have an intimate relationship with God, growing spiritually through regular quiet time in God's Word & prayer. (Spiritual Habits)	1 2 3 4 5
I respond to challenges with peace and faith to protect me from pain rather than anxiety and fear	1 2 3 4 5
I see myself more through God's eyes than my own	1 2 3 4 5
I avoid using addictive behaviors (food, television, busyness, etc.)	1 2 3 4 5
I am honoring God with my finances & my personal giving (budget) to God	1 2 3 4 5

Growing Total _____

DEVELOPING your SHAPE to serve others

I am expressing my gifts (S.H.A.P.E.) as a way of life at work and at home	1 2 3 4 5
I've attended the 301 CLASS, discovered my SHAPE & completed the SHAPE interview	1 2 3 4 5
I am serving in a regular (monthly or better) ministry to the church body	1 2 3 4 5
I am sharing responsibility within my small group by serving in a role	1 2 3 4 5
I am praying, discipling, or mentoring another person in the group or community	1 2 3 4 5

Developing Total _____

SHARING your life mission every day

I am actively praying for & cultivating relationships with unchurched friends & family	1 2 3 4 5
I am inviting seekers to church and sharing my spiritual story with them	1 2 3 4 5
I am participating in cross-cultural missions by discovering needs and praying for them	1 2 3 4 5
I am praying and considering where God can use my cross-culturally in the future	1 2 3 4 5
I am reproducing my life spiritually and/or praying for when this will happen	1 2 3 4 5

Sharing Total _____

SURRENDERING your life for God's pleasure

I am faithfully attending church worship services on the weekends	1 2 3 4 5
I have created a life mission statement and am seeking to fulfill it	1 2 3 4 5
I am growing in my personal worship to God through music & praise	1 2 3 4 5
I am surrendering my whole life by improving my exercise and nutrition	1 2 3 4 5
I am honoring God with every dimension of my life by balancing His purposes in my life	1 2 3 4 5

Surrendering Total _____

Just Beginning 0-5	FAIR 5-10	Getting Going 10-15	VERY GOOD 15-20	Well Developed 20-30

PERSONAL HEALTH LIFE PLAN

PURPOSES (Primary Questions)	POSSIBILITIES (Sample Plans)	PLANS (NEXT STEP) *Monthly Review*
CONNECTING WITH GOD'S FAMILY *Who am I connecting with spiritually?* *(Purpose of Fellowship)* Hebrews 10:24-25; Ephesians 2:19	• Attend my group more faithfully. • Schedule lunch with a group member. • Begin praying for a spiritual partner	
GROWING TO BE LIKE CHRIST *What is my next step for growth?* *(Purpose of Discipleship)* Colossians 1:28; Ephesians 4:15	• Commit to personal time with God three days a week. • Ask a friend for devotional accountability • Begin journaling my prayers	
DEVELOPING YOUR SHAPE TO SERVE OTHERS *Where am I serving in ministry?* *(Purpose of Serving)* Ephesians 4:11-13; 1 Corinthians 12:7; 1 Peter 3:10	• Begin praying for a personal ministry • Attend a gift discovery class • Serve together at a church event or in the community	
SHARING YOUR LIFE MISSION EVERYDAY *How am I shepherding another in Christ?* *(Purpose of Evangelism)* Matthew 28:19-20; Acts 20:24	• Start meeting for lunch with a seeker friend • Invite a non-Christian relative to church • Pray for and support an overseas missionary	
SURRENDERING YOUR HEART AS WORSHIP *How am I surrendering my heart today?* *(Purpose of Worship)* Romans 12:1&2; Psalm 27:6b	• Submit one area to God • Be honest about my struggles and hurt • Buy a music CD for worship my car and in the group	

SMALL GROUP HEALTH ASSESSMENT

CONNECTING with God's family

We are intentionally cultivating our relationships with Christian friends & spiritual mentors	1 2 3 4 5
We are cultivating authentic community by speaking truth in love and creating healthy boundaries	1 2 3 4 5
We are more loving, grace giving & forgiving to others than we were a year ago	1 2 3 4 5
We are resolving conflict with others in a Biblical manner, and supporting the leadership of this church family	1 2 3 4 5
We are willing to share our real needs for prayer and support with others	1 2 3 4 5

Connecting Total _____

GROWING to be like Christ

We have an intimate relationship with God, growing spiritually through regular quiet time in God's Word & prayer. (Spiritual Habits)	1 2 3 4 5
We respond to challenges with peace and faith to protect us from pain rather than anxiety and fear	1 2 3 4 5
We see ourselves more through God's eyes than our own	1 2 3 4 5
We avoid using addictive behaviors (food, television, busyness, etc.)	1 2 3 4 5
We are honoring God with our finances & our personal giving (budget) to God	1 2 3 4 5

Growing Total _____

DEVELOPING your SHAPE to serve others

We are expressing our gifts (S.H.A.P.E.) as a way of life at work and at home	1 2 3 4 5
We've attended the 301 CLASS, discovered our SHAPE & completed the SHAPE interview	1 2 3 4 5
We are serving in a regular (monthly or better) ministry to the church body	1 2 3 4 5
We are sharing responsibility within our small group by serving in a role	1 2 3 4 5
We are praying, discipling, or mentoring another person in the group or community	1 2 3 4 5

Developing Total _____

SHARING your life mission every day

We are actively praying for & cultivating relationships with unchurched friends & family	1 2 3 4 5
We are inviting seekers to church and sharing our spiritual story with them	1 2 3 4 5
We are participating in cross-cultural missions by discovering needs and praying for them	1 2 3 4 5
We are praying and considering on where God can use our cross-culturally in the future	1 2 3 4 5
We are reproducing our life spiritually and/or praying for when this will happen	1 2 3 4 5

Sharing Total _____

SURRENDERING your life for God's pleasure

We are faithfully attending church worship services on the weekends	1 2 3 4 5
We have created a life mission statement and are seeking to fulfill it	1 2 3 4 5
We are growing in our personal worship to God through music & praise	1 2 3 4 5
We are surrendering our whole life by improving our exercise and nutrition	1 2 3 4 5
We are honoring God with every dimension of our life by balancing His purposes in our life	1 2 3 4 5

Surrendering Total _____

Just Beginning	FAIR	Getting Going	VERY GOOD	Well Developed
0-5	5-10	10-15	15-20	20-30

SMALL GROUP HEALTH PLAN

PURPOSES (Primary Questions)	POSSIBILITIES (Sample Plans)	PLANS (OUR NEXT STEP) Monthly Review
CONNECTING WITH GOD'S FAMILY *(Purpose of Fellowship)* *Hebrews 10:24-25; Ephesians 2:19* *Who are we connecting deeper with relationally?*	• Host a family barbeque • Pass around the CLASS sign-up sheet • Share our extended life stories	
GROWING TO BE LIKE CHRIST *(Purpose of Discipleship)* *Colossians 1:28; Ephesians 4:15* *What is our next step for spiritual growth?*	• Commit as a group to regular quiet times • Memorize one verse a month • Read a book on spiritual growth	
DEVELOPING YOUR SHAPE TO SERVE OTHERS *(Purpose of Serving)* *Ephesians 4:11-13; 1 Corinthians 12:7; 1 Peter 3:10* *Where are we serving together?*	• Share ministry involvement stories and plans • Pray for everyone to find a ministry by the fall season • Serve together at Easter	
SHARING YOUR LIFE MISSION EVERYDAY *(Purpose of Evangelism)* *Matthew 28:19-20; Acts 20:24* *How can we share Christ and fulfill our Life Mission in the world?*	• Pray for your family and friends • Share plans and progress for inviting people to Easter • Pray for the African mission team	
SURRENDERING OUR LIFE AS WORSHIP *(Purpose of Worship)* *Romans 12:1&2; Psalm 27:6b* *How can I surrender my life today?*	• Faithfully use the prayer/praise list • Experiment with group worship • Host a communion service this quarter	

LIFETOGETHER CHURCH HEALTH PLAN EXAMPLE

PURPOSES (Scriptural Mandates)	PRIORITIES (Spiritual Direction)	PLANS Specific Steps	PROGRESS (Seasonal Evaluation)
CONNECTING (FELLOWSHIP)			
Bring them into Membership • Connect • Care • Champion • Communicate	• Connecting the unconnected in groups • Promoting Church Membership • Celebrating Baptisms	• Launch new small groups 3 times a year • Promote the church membership class • Send invitations to community for Easter & Christmas	
GROW (DESCIPLESHIP)			
Build them up to Maturity • Habits / Spiritual Disciplines • Small groups • God's word in their lives	• Applying the five purposes • Providing help to those with addictions or life issues • Discipling people in Small Groups	• Align the sermons with small group study on purposes • Offer recovery groups • Share testimonies of life change in small groups	
DEVELOP (SERVICE)			
Train them for ministry • Discovered Shape • Serving on a regular basis • Sharing in small group roles	• Assist people in discovering their S.H.A.P.E. • Connecting people to serve in Church ministries • Developing leaders of small groups	• Offer Small group leader training on discovering your gifts • Hold ministry fair, • Ask all groups to champion Host/leader rotation	
SHARE (EVANGELISM)			
Send them out for Mission • Life Mission • Evangelism • Cross-Cultural	• Reaching Seekers • Raising volunteer mission teams • Small group mission projects	• Groups host summer celebrations and invite neighbors and friends • Groups do a mission project this summer • Host "each one reach one" event.	
SURRENDER (WORSHIP)			
Surrender through magnification • Personal Worship • Small Group Worship • Corporate Worship	• Worshiping on the Weekends • Worshiping in Small groups • Worshiping in individual's lives daily	• Develop a weekend worship team including a service programmer • Promote all groups practicing worship and DVD videos • Provide retreats for small group leaders and members	

LIFETOGETHER CHURCH HEALTH PLAN

PURPOSES *(Scriptural Mandates)*	PRIORITIES *(Spiritual Direction)*	PLANS *Specific Steps*	PROGRESS *(Seasonal Evaluation)*
CONNECTING **(FELLOWSHIP)**			
Bring them into Membership • Connect • Care • Champion • Communicate			
GROW **(DESCIPLESHIP)**			
Build them up to Maturity • Habits / Spiritual Disciplines • Small groups • God's word in their lives			
DEVELOP **(SERVICE)**			
Train them for ministry • Discovered Shape • Serving on a regular basis • Sharing in small group roles			
SHARE **(EVANGELISM)**			
Send them out for Mission • Life Mission • Evangelism • Cross-Cultural			
SURRENDER **(WORSHIP)**			
Surrender through magnification • Personal Worship • Small Group Worship • Corporate Worship			

CHURCH HEALTH ASSESSMENT

CONNECTING with God's family

We are intentionally cultivating our relationships with Christian friends & spiritual mentors	1 2 3 4 5
We are cultivating authentic community by speaking truth in love and creating healthy boundaries	1 2 3 4 5
We are more loving, grace giving & forgiving to others than we were a year ago	1 2 3 4 5
We are resolving conflict with others in a Biblical manner, and supporting the leadership of this church family	1 2 3 4 5
We are willing to share our real needs for prayer and support with others	1 2 3 4 5

Connecting Total _____

GROWING to be like Christ

We have an intimate relationship with God, growing spiritually through regular quiet time in God's Word & prayer. (Spiritual Habits)	1 2 3 4 5
We respond to challenges with peace and faith to protect us from pain rather than anxiety and fear	1 2 3 4 5
We see ourselves more through God's eyes than our own	1 2 3 4 5
We avoid using addictive behaviors (food, television, busyness, etc.)	1 2 3 4 5
We are honoring God with our finances & our personal giving (budget) to God	1 2 3 4 5

Growing Total _____

DEVELOPING your SHAPE to serve others

We are expressing our gifts (S.H.A.P.E.) as a way of life at work and at home	1 2 3 4 5
We've attended the 301 CLASS, discovered our SHAPE & completed the SHAPE interview	1 2 3 4 5
We are serving in a regular (monthly or better) ministry to the church body	1 2 3 4 5
We are sharing responsibility within our small group by serving in a role	1 2 3 4 5
We are praying, discipling, or mentoring another person in the group or community	1 2 3 4 5

Developing Total _____

SHARING your life mission every day

We are actively praying for & cultivating relationships with unchurched friends & family	1 2 3 4 5
We are inviting seekers to church and sharing our spiritual story with them	1 2 3 4 5
We are participating in cross-cultural missions by discovering needs and praying for them	1 2 3 4 5
We are praying and considering on where God can use our cross-culturally in the future	1 2 3 4 5
We are reproducing our life spiritually and/or praying for when this will happen	1 2 3 4 5

Sharing Total _____

SURRENDERING your life for God's pleasure

We are faithfully attending church worship services on the weekends	1 2 3 4 5
We have created a life mission statement and are seeking to fulfill it	1 2 3 4 5
We are growing in our personal worship to God through music & praise	1 2 3 4 5
We are surrendering our whole life by improving our exercise and nutrition	1 2 3 4 5
We are honoring God with every dimension of our life by balancing His purposes in our life	1 2 3 4 5

Surrendering Total _____

Just Beginning 0-5	FAIR 5-10	Getting Going 10-15	VERY GOOD 15-20	Well Developed 20-30

SMALL GROUP LEADER LESSONS
WEEKLY LEADERSHIP TIPS

(Review each lesson and regularly share them with your group, apprentice or co-leader)

*And David shepherded them with integrity of heart;
with skillful hands he led them.*
Psalm 78:73

David provides us with a model of a leader who has a heart for God, a desire to shepherd God's people, and a willingness to develop the skills of a leader. The following is a series of practical tips for new and existing small group leaders. These principles and practices have cultivated thousands of examples of healthy, balanced groups over time.

1. Don't Leave Home without it: A Leader's Prayer
"The prayer of a righteous man [or woman] is powerful and effective." (James 5:16) From the very beginning of this study, why not commit to a simple prayer of renewal in your heart and in the hearts of your members? Take a moment right now and write a simple prayer as you begin:
Father, help me

_____
_____
_____
_____

2. **Pay it Now or Pay it Later: Group Conflict**
Most leaders and groups avoid conflict, but healthy groups are willing to do what it takes to learn and grow through conflict. Much group conflict can be avoided if the leader lets the group openly discuss and decide its direction using the Small Group Agreement. Healthy groups are alive. Conflict is a sign of maturity, not mistakes. Sometimes you may need to get outside counsel, but don't be afraid. Look at conflict as an opportunity to grow, and always confront it so it doesn't create a cancer that can kill the group over time. (Matthew 18:15-20)

3. **Lead from Weakness**
The apostle Paul said that God's power was made perfect in Paul's weakness (2 Corinthians 12:9). This is clearly the opposite of what most leaders think, but it provides the most powerful model of humility, authority, and spiritual power. It was Jesus' way at the cross. So share your struggles along with your successes, confess your sins to one another along with your celebrations, and ask for prayer for yourself along with praying for others.
God will be pleased, and your group will grow deeper. If you humble yourself under God's mighty hand, He will exalt you at the proper time (Matthew 23:12).

4. **What Made Jesus Cry: A Leader's Focus**
In Matthew 9:35-38, Jesus looked at the crowds following him and saw them as sheep without a

shepherd. He was moved with compassion, because they were "distressed and downcast" (NASB); the NIV says they were "harassed and helpless." The Greek text implies that he was moved to the point of tears.

Never forget that you were once one of those sheep yourself. We urge you to keep yourself and your group focused, not just inwardly on each other, but also outwardly to people beyond your group. Jesus said, "Follow me . . . and I will make you fishers of men." (Matthew 4:19) We assume that you and your group are following him. So how is your fishing going? As leader, you can ignite in your group Jesus' compassion for outsiders. For his sake, keep the fire burning!

5. **Prayer Triplets**
Prayer triplets can provide a rich blessing to you and many others. At the beginning or end of your group meeting, you can gather people into prayer triplets to share and pray about three non-Christian friends. This single strategy will increase your group's evangelistic effectiveness considerably. Be sure to get an update on the plans and progress from each of the circles. You need only ten minutes at every other meeting—or at least once a month. At first, some of your members may feel overwhelmed at the thought of praying for non-Christians. We've been there! But you can be confident that over time they will be renewed in their heart for lost people and experience the blessing of giving birth to triplets.

6. **Race against the Clock**
When your group grows in size or your members begin to feel more comfortable talking, you will inevitably feel as though you're racing against the clock. You may already know the feeling well. The good news is that there are several simple things that can help your group stick to your agreed schedule. The time crunch is actually a sign of relational and spiritual health, so pat yourselves on the back. Check in with the group to problem-solve, because they feel the tension as well. You could begin your meeting a little early or ask for a later ending time.

If you split up weekly into circles of three to four people for discussion, you will double the amount of time any one person can share. Appoint a timekeeper to keep the group on schedule. Remind everyone to give brief answers. Be selective in the number of questions you try to discuss. Finally, planning the time breaks in your booklet before the group meeting begins can really keep you on track.

7. **All for One and One for All: Building a Leadership Team**
The statement, "Together Everybody Accomplishes More," (TEAM) is especially true in small groups. The Bible clearly teaches that every member is a minister. Be sure to empower the group to share weekly facilitation as well as other responsibilities, and seek to move every player onto a team over time. Don't wait for people to volunteer, because that probably won't happen! From the outset, try to get everybody involved. The best way to get people in the game is to have the group suggest who would serve best on what team and in what role. See the Healthy Small Group Team feature on for several practical suggestions. You could also talk to people individually ask for volunteers in the group, but don't miss this opportunity to develop every group member and build a healthy and balanced group over time.

8. **Healthy Groups Produce Healthy Lives: A Leader's Goal**
As you undertake this new curriculum, especially if this is your first time as a leader, make sure you begin with the end in mind. You may have heard the phrase, "If you aim at nothing, you'll hit it every time." It's vital for your group members to review their spiritual health by using the Personal Health Assessment and Personal Health Plan. You'll do part of the Health Assessment with your group in Session 2, and share your results with spiritual partners for support and accountability.

Each member will also set one goal for thirty days. The goal will be tied to the purpose you are studying in this particular guide. We strongly encourage you to go even further and do the entire Health Assessment together. Then during another group session (or on their own), members can set a goal for each of the other four purposes.

Pairing up with spiritual partners will offer invaluable support for that area of personal growth. Encourage partners to pray for one another in the area of their goals. Have partners gather at least three times during the series to share their progress and plans. This will give you and the group the best results. In order for people to follow through with their goals, you'll need to lead with vision and modeling. Take the entire Health Assessment yourself, and give some serious thought to realistic goals that God would have you reach. Share your goals with the group, and update them on how the steps you're taking have been affecting your spiritual life. If you share your progress and plans, others will follow in your footsteps.

9. **Discover the Power of Pairs**
The best resolutions get swept aside by busyness and forgetfulness, which is why it's important for group members to have support as they pursue a spiritual goal. Have them pair up with spiritual partners in Session 2, or encourage them to seek out a Christian coworker or personal mentor. If they do this, they will grow like never before. This simple prescription can increase everyone's success rate by a factor of ten. You can promise that they'll never be the same if they simply commit to supporting each other with prayer and encouragement on a weekly basis.

It's best to start with one goal in the area of greatest need. Most of the time that area will be either evangelism, or consistent time with the Father in prayer and in reading the scriptures. Cultivating time with God is the place to start; if group members are already doing this, they can move on to a second and third area of growth.

You just need a few victories in the beginning. Have spiritual partners check in together at the beginning or end of each group meeting. Ask them to support each other with phone calls, coffee times and email messages during the week. Trust us on this one, you'll see them grow like never before.

10. **Don't Lose Heart: A Leader's Vision**
You are a strategic player in the heavenly realm. Helping a few others grow in Christ could put you squarely in the sights of Satan himself. I Corinthians 15:58 (NASB) says, "Be steadfast, immovable, always abounding in the work of the Lord." Leading a group is not always going to be easy.

Here are the keys to longevity and lasting joy as a leader:

a. Be sure to refuel your soul as you give of yourself to others. We recommend that you ask a person to meet with you for personal coaching and encouragement. When asked (over coffee or lunch) to support someone in leadership, nine out of ten people say, "I'd love to!" So why not ask?

b. Delegate responsibilities after the first meeting. Doing so will help group members grow, and it will give you a break as well.

c. Most importantly, cultivating your own walk with God puts you on the offensive against Satan and increases the joy zone for everyone in your life. Make a renewed decision right now to make this happen. Don't give Satan a foothold in your heart; there is simply too much at stake.

SMALL GROUP LEADERSHIP 101

Group Leadership 101 (Top Ten Ideas for New Facilitators)

Congratulations! You have responded to the call to help shepherd Jesus' flock. There are few other tasks in the family of God that surpass the contribution you will be making. As you prepare to lead—whether it is one session or the entire series—here are a few thoughts to keep in mind. We encourage you to read these and review them with each new discussion leader before he or she leads.

1. Remember that you are not alone. God knows everything about you, and he knew that you would be asked to lead your group. Even though you may not feel ready to lead, this is common for all good leaders. Moses, Solomon, Jeremiah, or Timothy—they *all* were reluctant to lead. God promises, "Never will I leave you; never will I forsake you" (Hebrews 13:5). Whether you are leading for one evening, for several weeks, or for a lifetime, you will be blessed as you serve.

2. Don't try to do it alone. Pray right now for God to help you build a healthy leadership team. If you can enlist a co-leader to help you lead the group, you will find your experience to be much richer. This is your chance to involve as many people as you can in building a healthy group. All you have to do is call and ask people to help—you'll be surprised at the response.

3. Just be yourself. If you won't be you, who will? God wants to use your unique gifts and temperament. Don't try to do things exactly like another leader; do them in a way that fits you! Just admit it when you don't have an answer and apologize when you make a mistake. Your group will love you for it!— and you'll sleep better at night

4. Prepare for your meeting ahead of time. Review the session and the leader's notes, and write down your responses to each question. Pay special attention to exercises that ask group members to do something other than engage in discussion. These exercises will help your group *live* what the Bible teaches, not just talk about it. Be sure you understand how an exercise works, and bring any necessary supplies (such as paper or pens) to your meeting.

If the exercise employs one of the items in the appendix (such as the Purpose-Driven Life Health Assessment), be sure to look over that item so you'll know how it works. Finally, review "Read Me First" on pages 11–14 so you'll remember the purpose of each section in the study.

5. Pray for your group members by name. Before you begin your session, go around the room in your mind and pray for each member by name. You may want to review the prayer list at least once a week. Ask God to use your time together to touch the heart of every person uniquely. Expect God to lead you to whomever he wants you to encourage or challenge in a special way. If you listen, God will surely lead!

6. When you ask a question, be patient. Someone will eventually respond. Sometimes people need a moment or two of silence to think about the question, and if silence doesn't bother you, it won't bother anyone else. After someone responds, affirm the response with a simple "thanks" or "good job." Then ask, "How about somebody else?" or "Would someone who hasn't shared like to add anything?" Be sensitive to new people or reluctant members who aren't ready to say, pray, or do anything. If you give them a safe setting, they will blossom over time.

7. Provide transitions between questions. When guiding the discussion, always read aloud the transitional paragraphs and the questions. Ask the group if anyone would like to read the paragraph or Bible passage. Don't call on anyone, but ask for a volunteer, and then be patient until someone begins. Be sure to thank the person who reads aloud.

8. Break up into small groups each week, or they won't stay. If your group has more than seven people, we strongly encourage you to have the group gather in discussion circles of three or four people during the GROWING or SURRENDERING sections of the study. With a greater opportunity to talk in a small circle, people will connect more with the study, apply more quickly what they're learning, and ultimately get more out of it. A small circle also encourages a quiet person to participate and tends to minimize the effects of a more vocal or dominant member. And it can help people feel more loved in your group. When you gather again at the end of the section, you can have one person summarize the highlights from each circle. Small circles are also helpful during prayer time. People who are unaccustomed to praying aloud will feel more comfortable trying it with just two or three others. Also, prayer requests won't take as much time, so circles will have more time to actually pray. When you gather back with the whole group, you can have one person from each circle briefly update everyone on the prayer requests. People are more willing to pray in small circles if they know that the whole group will hear all the prayer requests.

9. Rotate facilitators weekly. At the end of each meeting, ask the group who should lead the following week. Let the group help select your weekly facilitator. You may be perfectly capable of leading each time, but you will help others grow in their faith and gifts if you give them opportunities to lead. You can use the Small Group Calendar on page 69 to fill in the names of all six meeting leaders at once if you prefer.

10. One final challenge (for new or first-time leaders): Before your first opportunity to lead, look up each of the five passages listed below. Read each one as a devotional exercise to help prepare yourself with a shepherd's heart. Trust us on this one. If you do this, you will be more than ready for your first meeting.

Matthew 9:36
1 Peter 5:2-4
Psalm 23
Ezekiel 34:11–16
1 Thessalonians 2:7–8, 11–12

GREAT CONVERSATION STARTERS

Good questions draw people in and keep a conversation flowing. Be on the lookout for good questions. Below are some suggestions:

1. What's your preferred ice cream flavor? Where do you usually enjoy it?
2. How many brothers and sisters do you have? What is your birth order?
3. Which do you prefer: the hustle and bustle of city life or the quiet and serenity of country life? Why?
4. What's your all-time favorite meal, and how often do you enjoy it?
5. What's one of your nicknames? What do you prefer to be called?
6. As a child, what was your idea of fun?
7. What's a phrase your parents often said to you as a child that you promised yourself you'd never say, but now you catch yourself saying all the time?
8. As a kid, what did you want to grow up to be?
9. What's one of your hobbies?
10. What books have made a big impact on you?
11. What was the most recent compliment that surprised and delighted you?
12. What's something about yourself that you hope will never change?
13. Are you more of a rule breaker or a rule keeper? Why?
14. Would you describe yourself as an extrovert or an introvert? Explain.
15. What's your dream job?
16. What's one of your greatest achievements?
17. What one word sums up your high school experience? Why?
18. What's the first thing that comes to your mind when you hear the word "fun"?
19. What are you a "natural" at doing? What skills have you just always had?
20. How often do you leisurely eat a meal with friends?

BUILDING LIFETOGETHER CASE STUDIES

CASE STUDY: A TREMENDOUS GAIN
GARY KENDALL, INDIAN CREEK CHURCH, NEAR KANSAS CITY

Chris: Gary let's go ahead and start with you. Would you just share for a few minutes about your church and about where you were and how you got connected with Brett? And kind of what you see as the future?

Gary: I would be glad to Chris. We were beginning a capital campaign last fall. And we knew as we were beginning the campaign we wanted it to be more than just a campaign to raise money. We had been through the 40 Days of Purpose a year before and experienced a great fruitful time in that. We began to wonder if it was possible to combine those two together. Our consultant in that day was a man named David Grubbs who knows Brett and knows about Life Together. As David was talking to us he said, "I think the thread that might bind all of this together would be to build it around the small group ministry. He began to share about Life Together, began to talk about that and the curriculum. We caught a vision about what could happen if we would begin to employ the idea that was a new concept to me that we could have 100% of people who were attending our morning worship into small groups. I like any pastor would say that would be the goal. But reality would say we'll come somewhere south of that. But as we got hooked up with Brett and Life Together and began to look at doing things a different way, I began to believe that this is a real possibility for us.

Let me just cut right to the chase on numbers. Anything that Brett wants me to pick up on that I might have left out I'd be glad to cover but we're a church on a typical Sunday morning anywhere between 1000 and 1200 in total attendance – 650 of them are adults – in three different worship services. We set a goal of a minimum of 65 groups. In other words, one for every 10. Plus Brett convinced us we should shoot for 130% because there are people who typically aren't in church on a given Sunday and there are seekers out there. So we set a goal of 83 groups. Going into this time we had 24 groups at right about 250 people – adults in small groups on a regular basis. At the end of the campaign, by the time we reached the end of November, we didn't quite hit the 65 number but we were close to it. We were at 59. Then we also were able to identify over 30 other small groups that weren't doing just the Life Together curriculum. So all together we had almost 500 adults in small groups. I'm positive that not only did our small group Bible studies face a huge kind of growth because of the emphasis on small groups but it helped every other group in the church. Now we're taking another run at the mountain. We're going back to the 83 number again as we head into Easter. The amazing thing for us was that out of all the groups that we started, we had over 100% increase, out of all the groups we started when we did the sign up for the 2nd phase we only lost one, which just amazed me because we have all these new leaders and we only lost one. So we had some atrophy over the holidays and now we're taking another run at it before Easter. A tremendous gain. It really exceeded what I would have imagined that we could do.

Chris: So do you think this is going to have any impact on your capital campaign?

Gary: Oh, we did well on our capital campaign. Our goal was to raise at least 4 million and it was a church of 650 adults was a challenging total. We came somewhere just short of 5 million. So we hit that too. The best part was we had a baptism service with 83 people that were baptized. So I think the small groups were the thread for the campaign the 40 Days of Purpose. It's something that's lasted well beyond the fall and it's going to be the way we do ministry here at Indian Creek. So I'm grateful for the coaching we received because I know we couldn't have done it without that.

CASE STUDY: CONNECTING EVERYONE

by Roger Funk, Faith Bible Chapel, Denver CO

We're Faith Bible Chapel, a church of about 4000 in a suburb of Denver, Colorado. I was on a call just like this in January of 2003. I was so excited with what Brett shared. We signed on to do a series of coaching calls with Brett and Life Together. It dramatically changed my life, my ministry, our church.

Brett: You actually came to Christ as a result of these conferences.

Roger: I came to Christ on the first call! Brett's passion for discipleship and small groups. We were stuck for years, this includes small group pastors before me of about 30 small groups. After last fall we did about a 400% increase up to 120. We multiplied all sorts of new hosts and new coaches and new leaders who had never been part before and are now stand out stars. We had about a third of the people in attendance in our groups were from the community not from our church. One of the things we found out as we were getting ready to go from the initial 6 weeks into the next 6 weeks. People were asking the groups, Do you want to continue? Groups that were almost 100% community were the ones who absolutely did not want to stop, no way, let's keep going, let's do the next study. It's phenomenal. They're still going to this day. It'll give them a word of God for the first time ever in their entire lives. We have a 101 class Discovering Your Ministry. Prior to that the number of people that would be in off campus small group before that got in 101 was pretty much zero percent. Now we're averaging about 15%. They're not only people joining our group but also bringing people into the church through our groups which has never happened before. So we're thrilled. Brett, Cynthia and the team have been an absolute tremendous and wonderful help to us. I'd love to see as many churches as possible receive the same benefits we did.

Chris: So when you were on those coach calls you got some good pointers?

Roger: Phenomenal. I mean the first 6 weeks which back then was called Building Life Together absolutely blew all of my paradigms apart and gave me a whole new view of the church and small groups and discipleship. It just exploded what I even believed was possible through my ministry or our church's ministry. It wasn't a pipedream. We've seen it happen.

CASE STUDY: PUSHING THE PEDAL DOWN AFTER 40 DAYS OF PURPOSE

By: Terri Cobb, Valencia Hills Community Church

We did it this weekend too. It's for the summer. Our senior pastor asked from the pulpit and we got 75 people.

75 people to do what?
75 people agreed to be hosts.
That's a wow!

B: How Big is your church, Terri?

Terri: We usually have about 650 adults and children, everybody.

B: Get rid of all the kids for just conversation sake. I have five of them so I can say that.

Terri: If we got rid of the kids, I'd say 450 adults.

B: Just do the math guys. That's the first weekend. She's got 15% that said yes. What if she plugged it for 2 more weeks?

Terri: He's going to plug this next week for the 3-week session. We're starting ion the 21st and he wants it to culminate on good Friday. Then on Easter we're kicking of Life Together.

B: Oh, you're using our curriculum?

Terri: Yes, for Easter.

B: Which one?

Terri: Growing.

B: That's great. I didn't know.

: How many people did you have in small groups prior to this?

Terri: Right now I have 30 groups. So I have about 350 adults.

: Wow!

B: What it would be helpful to do… I'm going to send you a survey, Terri. Called the Host Home Survey. I want you to send it to every one of these hosts. It is a tool that I use to screen, to make sure you're not getting ax murders in the thing. But I want you then to send it to all your hosts and they will give you... it's functionally like an application as well as a confirmation. What you kind of want to do is give them a temporary blessing. Just do the thing for 6 weeks. But it is critical when you bring those people into training that you ask them all to bring in a co-host. Never again use the word apprentice. But bring in a co-host. That co-host will help them land that deal then rotate leadership on the 2nd or 3rd week and have your husband to challenge them to do that from the pulpit. That will build a healthy group and turn on what I call the crock pot and your fall, Terri, will be unlike no fall in the history of any church your size. You took the little seed of stuff we did last week and turned it into a complete victory, harvest, a whole field. It's amazing.

Terri: By faith we ordered 100 of The Passion, so my husbands' going to push again this Sunday and get 25 more.

B: You guys, this is awesome. I love it. Terri, you've got more faith than me.

Terri: I figured human reasoning we could double it. If we had 30, double would be 60. That's safe and that leaves our a faith factor.

B: You guys, this is a woman who I met at a seminar about 4-5 weeks ago. She said, This sounds crazy. What about all these non Christians? This thing is never going to fly. We've got a young church. And look at what she just did by the grace of God. Any questions you guys want to ask her real quick. We're about 10 minutes over and I'm so excited I want to keep going but I've got to honor the time.

: I think it's going to go great because when we did the 40 Days of Purpose in the fall we asked people from our existing groups and people from our church, we had 24 existing groups, and we got 70 people to sign up to be hosts when we did that in the fall. This is great. That's going to go really well for you.

B: The thing that I'm moved by is that most of the pastors that have 40 Days they put the peddle down. They do their best to follow the path but then they pull off the pedal. The fact that you pushed the pedal back down, you're following the coaching of a guy named Jimmie Davison the very first pastor that I worked with on all this stuff. He said, "Brett, I lost about 35-50% of my groups after I put close to 100% in." I said, "What would you say to Paul, senior pastor to a church that is headed for the same thing?" He said I'd do two things. I'd keep my eye on the small group ball more because I didn't realize the tool that it is and should be in the church, especially house to house and temple courts. I just didn't realize how significant it was. Number 2, I did not keep challenging people to go deeper with the purposes in the context of community and to keep recruiting people to open their homes and challenging people to be able to do life together, and not just do a series together. He said, I'm having to do a little bit of backup but it's similar to what Joey O'Conner said. They had 100 groups. That church was only about 1200-1300 when they had 100 groups. I was with Joey's predecessor at a conference 8 years ago. They were looked on as a model. If you don't have a Peter in your cause Paul you're got somebody who's a champion of this, like Terri you're serving right now, the thing will lose its steam. All of you are headed for the Grand Canyon of small groups which is called summer. But we worked with a church local called Mariners and we did about 4 or 5 things that insured that they only lost – you're always going to lose some – they only lost 15%. So do not back off. If you do not do what Terri does, at least in a Pilot for or what Peter and Paul just said they did, please you are missing out on opportunity. I want everybody to have a baby step win at least if not a big win like Terri and Paul just did. Could I challenge you guys to do that? You are on this pilot. Let's not hold back. If you need your senior pastor on next week, whatever it takes. If your senior pastor and you've got other plans, just at least do it with some of the existing groups. Just try a test drive in Sunday school and talk and challenge the existing group leaders like Gary Kendall did. Because you will have more confidence going into the fall.

Terri could you pray for the faith of all of us to multiply as yours and your husband?

Terri: Dear heavenly Father, I just pray that you would just use each of us. I know that myself and perhaps others we're entering uncharted waters. Lord we need Your wisdom, we need Your guidance. Help us to have big faith. We're just praying with expectation that You will do immeasurably more than we could ever hope for or imagine. I just pray, dear God, that You would send us leaders who would be faithful and aren't crazy and lack skills. But as we entrust our members the people will stay, we're just trusting that You watch over us and You give us the faith and the trust that we need to believe in you More. In Christ's name we pray.

B: It's always a blessing. I love being with you.

CASE STUDY: DISCOVERING COMMUNITY
Walt Kallestad, Community Church of Joy

Everyone at Community Church of Joy (CCOJ) in Glendale, Arizona, knew that God was moving in their church and preparing them for something new. They just didn't know what it was.

With this spirit of expectancy, Dr. Walt Kallestad decided to take a sabbatical. He and his wife, Mary, set this time aside specifically for prayer and seeking God's will for their next step. They visited churches in Africa and Europe, studied and read, and spent hours on their knees. During their travels, they were deeply impacted by a small church in Sheffield, England, that was forced to meet in homes because the building they had once met in had been condemned. This passionate church was based on a house-church model right out of Acts 2.

The Kallestads came back from the sabbatical with a clear vision of God's plans for CCOJ: Small groups would become the crux of how they connected their members and their community.

God had been setting the wheels in motion for this change even before Pastor Walt left on his sabbatical. Their church had always had a few small groups, but most of them had not continued over time so they ended up having only a handful meeting at any given time.

Before he left, Pastor Walt had staff member Rev. Dottie Escobedo-Frank contact Lifetogether in California. She flew out to join their gathering of leaders from several churches at the forefront of small group development. This was the beginning of their partnership with Lifetogether.

When they embarked on this journey, they knew small groups were going to be a *part* of their plan for the future, they didn't know that it would become their whole new way of doing church. With the Kallestads' return, small groups went from being viewed as a valuable new program to being central to what the Lord was going to do in their community. Now it's "not about small groups happening in one program area," says Escobedo-Frank. "It's about this being a whole transition for the church. The whole church, all the staff, everybody is getting aligned with this idea."

Even though they are still early in this transition, the response from the members has already been incredibly positive. The truth that God actually created them to be in community continues to resonate with them. Escobedo-Frank says members regularly come to her saying everything from "I'm lonely. I need to be a part of a group" to "I finally found a way to connect" to "I've never been asked to serve before." Members are really responding to the call to get into community.

CASE STUDY: THE POWER OF "40 DAYS OF PURPOSE"

Skip Parsons, Bible Baptist Worship Center

I just have to share with you what God has done and is doing in our church.

In early June of last year, the Hope for America Foundation (a Christian foundation based in Cape Giradeau, MO) contacted us to see if we would allow them to use our campus for a week long crusade to reach the Western Kentucky area. They said they had Jerry Falwell, John Hagee, James Merit, and Adrian Rogers already lined up. After discussions, it was decided that we would allow it. The crusade was scheduled for September 15 - September 20.

In mid July I was handed a packet of information labeled 40 Days of Purpose. I was asked to look at it and give my opinion. I took it home with me that night and could not believe what I was reading. I immediately saw what it could do to the spiritual make up of our church. You see our church is a very traditional independent Baptist church. It was founded in 1959 from a split. The founding pastor left 15 months later to continue his education. Our senior pastor, Don Young has been the pastor since 1960. It has been said that we have had many pastors in that time, but only one man. In 1998, he recognized there was more to church than the way it was being done. Our church needed to change. Recognizing is one thing, implementing becomes the challenge.

I saw the 40 Days of Purpose as an opportunity to unite our people on a path of spiritual growth. Everyone was talking about how the crusade was going to have a major impact in our church and in the region. In reality, it was only a match being lit. Our 40 Days of Purpose campaign began exactly 3 weeks after the crusade. On Saturday, October 12, 2002, a bon fire was started!

We began with the hopes of getting 50-60% of our Sunday School adults involved. The first week of small groups saw a 110% involvement. WOW!! By the end of the campaign, people were saying, "do we have to stop meeting?"

Needless to say, the 40 Days of Purpose campaign has changed our church. Numbers cannot convey the excitement, the joy, and the desire to be closer to God in our people. We saw small groups ministering to people at Thanksgiving and Christmas that would have never been done so in the past. One group helped 3 families at Christmas. They were able to obtain gifts for the kids and grocery certificates from organizations in the community and additional food and money were given. It was awesome to witness the blessings of giving and receiving.

We are in the process of beginning our small groups for the year. We are using the Doing Life Together curriculum. Everyone is getting so excited about starting. We are going to have a big kick-off service similar to the simulcast of the 40 days. We took a little extra time to work with all the new people who are stepping up to lead a group. This past Wednesday training was a blessing. We had just over 100 people participating with some not able to make it.

God is changing the make up of our church. From the leadership to the visitor, we are in the process of transforming into a church that is not limited to its campus, but is reaching out into the community with a purpose. We still use our Sunday School and we are learning how to blend it with the small groups.

There are 2 other churches in Paducah that are going through the spring campaign this year. I have been meeting with both of them to help them with what we learned during our campaign. They are very excited already. The impact that this is going to have in our region is tremendous.

It reminds me of the old surfing movie "Endless Summer". They were in search of the perfect wave, one that did not end. I believe that wave has begun to break and it is not only going to impact our region, our state, and our country, but the entire world.

Thank you Brett for allowing God to use you and Rick Warren to reach out to churches like us. If it wasn't for your desire to see people come together in community, we would still be doing church the same old way.

CASE STUDY: WHAT A RIDE

Alan Buchanan, Highland Christian Fellowship, Virginia

I am writing you to tell you what an awesome time we are having at Highlands Fellowship with our small groups. Until 40 Days of Purpose our small groups were almost nonexistent. We would normally have only 5 or 6 small groups going at any one time. This is not very impressive when we look back and realize that we had 1100 to 1200 adults in regular attendance on any given weekend. The week after 9-11, we did a church wide launch of "Experiencing God" by Henry Blackaby. We had about 35 groups form and really struggled with leadership and how to care for the groups. Immediately following the Experiencing God study, we tried to keep all of the groups going by offering another study titled "If You Want to Walk on Water You've Got to Get Out of the Boat" by John Ortberg. After this study, we let our groups choose a curriculum of their own. Needless to say, without direction, they all pretty much dwindled away. Amazingly, the ones that were still alive as we approached summer, we killed them by giving them the summer off.

Then a remarkable thing happened for Highlands Fellowship. We were chosen to receive the North American Church Health Award to be presented at the Purpose-Driven Church Conference at Saddleback Church in May of 2002. Our pastor, Jimmie Davidson, has used the Purpose Driven model ever since he planted our church over seven years ago. People find it very interesting that he could maintain the vision even though he had never been to Saddleback or spoken to Rick Warren. Ten of us, including Pastor Jimmie and his wife, went to Saddleback in May. As a result of our attending this conference, Highlands Fellowship became completely committed to "40 Days of Purpose".

As we neared the launch date of "40 Days of Purpose" we began to realize what an impact this campaign was going to have on our church. About this same time you shared a vision with our pastor involving the use of part time division leaders. The vision included a grant to be made available to our church if we were willing to "test drive" the plan. We attended a conference in Oklahoma City in September and met with you, Bob Buford, several church leaders and potential division leaders from around the country. What timing! It never fails to amaze me how Gods' timing is always perfect.

Well, on October 12th and 13th we launched about 190 small groups. Praise God for revealing to Bob Buford and the Leadership Network how overwhelming this was going to be without proper leadership in place to take care of all of these small groups. Our small group program probably would have collapsed under the sheer weight of its success if we hadn't been encouraged to have division leaders in place.

It is interesting that our division leaders started out doing this as a part time job and have ended up having a relationship with their host home shepherd leaders. When they first started calling the leaders under their care they said they only talked a few minutes to get all of the information they needed. Now they are telling me that they may have a 30 or 40 minute conversation with each shepherd leader. They are also asking for prayer requests and praise reports at the end of each conversation and praying with the leader over the phone. They are actually having shepherd leaders call them during the week and wanting to know how they are doing and praying for them.

One of our division leaders has visited four different small groups on four different evenings this week. He said this had been an awesome experience for him. At one home, the group was doing the "hot seat" exercise. The group leader asked the division leader if he would pray with each member of the group after each had finished their turn in the hot seat. Our division leader was blown away. He went to the group to help out and walked away with a tremendous blessing.

A few weeks ago we were struggling with finding a way to place a large number of singles age 30-49 in a host home. Another one of our division leaders, over 50 years old and single, felt led to host this group. She has been overwhelmed with the blessings she has received and talks about "her" group all of the time.

Our Senior High Pastor, Deborah Whitt, has a small group meeting at her home. A young unsaved couple joined her group a few weeks ago. They had been attending Highlands Fellowship for two years but always arrived late and left early. They didn't even know our building had an elevator in it. They were in their third week of the study before they even realized that Deborah was a pastor at the church. They have accepted Christ, been baptized and have joined our church since first attending this small group.

There are so many stories of changed lives the past few months. Highlands Fellowship has also had a record year for baptisms and new members. WHAT A RIDE!!!!!

CASE STUDY: WHEN 100% CONNECTED FALLS SHORT OF GOD'S PLAN

Pastor John Rasz, The Vineyard, Wheeling, WV

Linda lay in bed recuperating from knee surgery. She had plenty of time to think. Well, that's about all she could do. As much as she wanted to go to church and participate in the weeks leading up to the 40 Days of Purpose, Linda could barely move out of bed.

She kept thinking about Pastor John's challenge to host a group for the 6-week campaign. But, how could that be possible? Linda began to pray. Though she couldn't get to the church to sign up group members, she prayed them into her group. When the week came to launch her group, Linda had 15 members. Seven of them were unchurched. One of those was her husband, who faithfully helped Linda prepare each week for her group meeting even though he had yet to surrender his life to Christ.

Prayer was in the formation of every group at The Vineyard in Wheeling, West Virginia. This 25-year-old church of 550 adults prayed and fasted about what God might do in and through their church as they studied *The Purpose Drive Life*. When Pastor John Rasz and Pastor of Small Groups Chris Figaretti presented a 3-week series on Community, they challenged each member of their church to open their hearts and their homes for six weeks to host a group.

Prior to this experience, their church, though they believed in small groups, only had five groups to show for it. "Church growth overtook the emphasis on small groups," says Pastor John. "It overwhelmed the infrastructure." The Lifetogether coaching program "helped us to develop a strategy through 40 days and beyond" remarks Chris.

On the first week of their campaign, 78 groups for adults and six groups for students began. They had groups for well over 100 percent of their adults.

The moment of awe came, however, shortly after the church had distributed their study guides. Each host was asked to take only enough study guides for their committed small group members. When Chris counted the remaining books, he discovered that only 50 copies remained from their order of 1000 study guides. The 78 groups had 950 members! Their church had gone from less than 10 percent connected in groups to 173 percent connected in only a matter of weeks.

How did that happen? Pastor John says that they made the invitation to host a group "as engageable as possible. We spoke to this in a singular voice. There were no competing agendas." All of the other programs and ministry drew their focus onto the 40 Days campaign.

While in previous years, small group leaders were carefully selected and thoroughly trained, this time around Pastor John changed the strategy. "We lowered the bar for people who have a heart for people" to host a group in their home.

Bob and Elaine were just those people. The couple made an arrangement with a local juvenile corrections center to release six of the girls to participate in the small group study each week. Ten other members of the church also joined the group. One of the girls gave her heart to Christ on the third day of the campaign.

Not only were members engaged to be hosts, but non-members were inquiring about small groups. "The fish were jumping into the boat," Chris exclaimed. One member named Penny prayed about hosting a group. She had never done this before, but was open to what God might do. Other teachers at her school "out of the blue" started asking Penny if she had heard of this book called *The Purpose-Driven Life*. "Coincidentally," that was the exact study that her church was about to begin. Penny started her group motivated by God and by her unchurched co-workers. Her group has 15 members. Eight of them don't go to church. In fact, 20 percent of the people in the church's small groups are unchurched.

The pastoral staff of the Vineyard, Wheeling attribute the response of their church to hosting, connecting and reaching out to a partnership they made themselves between using the Purpose-Driven 40 Days of Purpose campaign along with the Lifetogether Coaching Program and then, bathing the whole thing in prayer. "It was an intense focus in prayer" says Pastor John.

Chris admitted, "We knew the groups needed follow up after the 40 Days." That's why he urged his pastor to sign up for the Coaching Program. *The Purpose-Driven Life* gave them the platform to start. Lifetogether coaching gave them the strategies to sustain.

"The coaching program wasn't in our budget," but according to John Rasz "we wouldn't have the groups in our 40 Days campaign without Lifetogether."

CASE STUDY: SMALL CHURCH, BIG ON GROUPS

Pastor Bob, North Madison Church, Madison, IN

I'm not sure I can pinpoint 1 or 2 things that has launched such an incredible ministry tool and life changing adventure for our church we call Community Groups. I came on staff as the Sr. Pastor in May of 1998. NMCC was averaging 130 in Worship and 85 in Sunday School and 25 on Wednesday Bible Study. They had tried small groups in the past but they had no structure and one became a "what's wrong with our church?" group.

From the time I came on staff my goal was to cast the vision that we have so much potential as a church. In 5 years we jumped to 350 in Worship and 130 in Sunday School and 40 on Wednesdays. I knew that our growth was demanding us to grow smaller as we grew larger. I cast the vision with our leaders and after several "successes" they saw God's hand in what we were doing. They agreed to let me investigate the beginnings of small groups. (I decided to change the name, due to such a bad taste in their mouths from the last time to Community Groups) It fit since we cast the vision from the pulpit that an Acts 2 Prevailing Church committed to community in 4 ways:

    Community Worship: "…they continued to meet in the temple courts."
    Community Small groups: "…they met in homes."
    Community Ministry: "…they met each other's needs."
    Community Outreach: "…they found favor with everyone."

I cast the vision with our leaders, began my "E.F. Hutton" conversations with key church members (Maxwell's Laws of Leadership). We signed up with Brett and Life Together and began the conference calls. I began a sermon series called "Building Bridges" and from the pulpit cast the vision of the Community concept. I contacted 15 Leaders who I thought would be great H.O.S.T.s and took 3 Sundays to train them using Life Together and Willowcreek resources. 10 groups began with 3 leaders taking apprentice roles. Our Jr./Sr. High Pastor decided to launch community groups with the teens as well. He started 4. We began with the Beginning Life Together Series. We asked from the pulpit if people would give 6 weeks to try this new-to-us, but very biblical approach to fulfilling our 5 purposes. Our launch saw 145 adults being connected. During the 6 weeks, I had 2 Sundays where I asked for stories that fit with the series, "Building Bridges" and community groups. Those testimonies hit home as I purposely chose long-time members (who were apprehensive at first, and new members who were ready to go). We also were preparing for the 40 Days of Community.

When we began "Beginning Together" we were averaging 400 on Sunday morning. (September of 2004) and 145 in Community Groups. From the original 10, we birthed 18 more equaling 28 homes for 40 Days. I trained the new 18 H.O.S.T.s in just 2 hours with simple instructions and handouts with the vision "Just give God 6 weeks." Since beginning 40 Days we are now hitting 480 on Sundays and 238 in Community Groups! I send a weekly e-mail to all the hosts with encouraging ideas, and make it a point to make some kind of "touch" (phone call, visual on Sunday, etc.) every other week. We also had a "Mid Campaign Huddle" during week 4 to ask, "What's Hot?" "What's Not?" "What's Next?", and to cast the vision for our January launch. (We also are promoting a "Song of Solomon" marriage conference by giving each H.O.S.T. a DVD promo of the conference)

Right now, I am mentoring/training a couple to be "Community Coaches" for the H.O.S.T.s. They are watching as I do. Then we will do together. Then, they will do as I watch. And then they will pick another couple to watch them do as they do, while I refocus my energies to our next adventure.

As an established church, just new to the concept of Community Groups, I really am learning as I go as to what works and what doesn't. Here are some insights that happened by the grace of God:

- Key leaders caught the vision (As the Sr. Pastor, I bought into it and led it)
- 1st time success of Community Pilot Groups due to selective Community Group H.O.S.T.s (They needed to be successful to chart the way)
- Relational approach to leading H.O.S.T.s (not regimented in only having 1 way to do Community)
- Opening the door during the "40 Days Of Community" for anyone to be a H.O.S.T. and training them with the H.O.S.T.s from the previous 6 week campaign
- Sharing the "What's Hot?" stories through e-mail to all the other H.O.S.T.s during the week. It encouraged them and gave the groups ideas
- As the Sr. Pastor, being passionate about the whole process and sharing from the pulpit how my Community Group helps me

I don't know it this helps, and I know it's over 1 page. I guess it's the preacher in me. God bless and if you need any clarifications about the above, just let me know. Again, I'm humbled that you asked and I'm excited about our future here in Madison, IN!

CASE STUDY: MAKING THE ASK RECRUITING HOSTS DURING A 40 DAY CAMPAIGN

Gary Kendall, Sample Transcript

I know some of you know exactly what I'm about because you've experienced this kind of life giving community; some of you for 6 weeks, some of you 6 month, others for 6 years. You know you wouldn't do life any other way would you? You know this is the only way to live in community like this. And what I'm going to ask you next maybe radical, crazy, label it anything you want, I know this need is so universal that we need to extend it to everyone. In a sense, leave no one behind. And I want to join me, because my wife and I are going to do this too. Let's reach out to a circle of friends who don't you experience this kind of community. If you think with me for a moment you have friends like that in you life. Just look at your cell phone and you'll see a bunch of name and I bet there's a bunch of unconnected friends. You may sit every Saturday in the stands with the same soccer moms, you've gotten to know each other, you do parties together you cry together when the kids loose and you celebrate together when they win.

I'm just going to ask you to dream and ask yourself ask God, what would happen if you pose the question, Can we do life together for 6 weeks, let's intentionally talk about things that really matter. Ever find yourself going down the road in conversations and thinking this may be fun but it really doesn't get us anywhere in the end? I'm going to ask you to take a big step here and invited these people into life giving community. To share what you've experienced with them. Here's how I think of you. I think of you as a person who is a guide. Because what you've done is, you've walked down this path and found something that is life-giving so now you know the way. I'm going to ask you to take a 6 week vacation from your group and double-back and take the hand for someone, so they can come and find the kind of community that you've found. I know it's crazy, I know it's wild. Here's also what I know. I know that if you make the offer there are people who will accept. Your heart is going to grow a little, it's going to get wider. You're going to find some friends who are going to become life-long friends. You may find some friends that you'll share eternity with because you had the courage to reach out and ask.

I can imagine what some of you are thinking, when I make this kind of ask you're thinking, "well wait a minute, if we're about making community and we step-out to reach our hands to some friends then this is something we want to preserve, but now you're coming back pastor and saying 'I'd like you to reach your hands again'. The answer is 'yes', that's exactly what I'm asking, because where would you be if someone hadn't reached a hand to you? I know where I'd be, I'd be on the outside looking in. And this is not an either or thing, I'm not asking you to divorce your friends, I'm not asking you to forget your friends, I'm not asking you to ignore your friends. I'm just asking you to open up your hands just a little wider. I really believe you'll find ways to stay connected with these people who mean so much to you. Because what you have is special and you're not going to lose it in 6 weeks, but if you'll give 6 weeks, here's what you'll find. You'll find here's another circle of people who need to find what you've found and in 6 weeks worth of time they can be experiencing vital community like you experience it. Your heart is going to grow wider, you're not going to loose, your actually going to gain the circle is actually going to grow. I believe it can happen for you.

Now if were you, and I was listening to this ask, I would have one burning question and that would be "how, how are we going to do this?" Let me engage your thinking for just a moment to believe that God has already prepared the way for you in ways that you can't even imagine. Because, you see, the heart of God is already reaching out to the people around you, He's way ahead of us on this. I believe it can be a simple as saying, as we walk around in our everyday life, 'God, would you lead me to some divine appointments. Who is it that might be ready for this kind of invitation?' Think with me for a moment about the circles of influence we have, because we all have a circle of influence. I mentioned before soccer moms, or people you relate with through your kids. Or people on your cell phone list. And there are others, how about people in your neighborhood., some neighbors you talk across the fence or people down the street, you wave. And you know just enough about each other to know that there is a need there, there's a desire. And it's not just neighbors, sometimes it's family, other times it's people you went to high school with, you could really go far with this, but you have circles of influence, you have circles of infinity. In many cases if you were to reach out to these people they are ready to reciprocate because you already have this relationship built. All I'm asking you to do is to believe that God loves that person and He wants this message to get through you to them. Take the risk, share the love, reach out with this message and invite them into this circle, it might not be a big circle Jesus said, 'where two or three are gathered, there I am', He'll show-up. I'm asking you to reach out to your friends to a few of these people in your circle of influence and give God a chance to do something that could be life changing for all of you.

So here's what I'm going to ask you to do, inside your DVD there's a card, I want you to take that card, hold it up and whisper a prayer to God, And the prayer goes like this, "God would you go ahead of me and would you guide me to people who need this life-giving community ." And over the next couple of weeks take the opportunity to write some names on that card and turn it in and as soon as you do that you'll find people who are ready to support you in every way. With lots of support, coaching, people to pray with you, ideas. Here's the way I look at it I don't believe you can fail. God's right there with you and we're going to be surrounding you every step of the way. Now if you're a leader, we're going to ask you to lead, I'm leading and I'm doing this in my life and my family and I've done it before I'm going to do it again. I believe in it with all my heart, I'm going to give God a chance to do it again. If you're not a leader but you're part of a group go to the leader and say, "I'm in, Pastor is off on one of his crazy 'asks' again, there he goes again, but say, 'I'm just crazy enough to go with him, I'm going to give this a chance, let's do it in our group". And so I want to encourage everybody with 100% participation,,,this thought's been going thru my mind, "no one stands alone". God find one other person, if you're a couple go find another couple to go with you, Jesus sent the disciples out two by two, find one other person go out and give God a chance. Turn in that card and I believe when you do your life is gets real exciting in a hurry, and also you are on the verge of some great things happening. There'll some new learning, some new experiences and some new friends. So let me net it out for you: go find some one that you'd like to do life together with, and ask, give God a chance and the rest will become next year's history.

As I close I want you to meet my friend, Pete is a man I met last year doing this same thing that I'm asking you to do. Pete first became a friend then he became a brother, now he's a leader. I want you to met Pete, because his story could become your story.

CASE STUDY: FROM 0 TO 60 IN THIRTY DAYS
HOW TO CONNECT YOUR ENTIRE CONGREGATION INTO GROUPS

Jimmie Davidson, Highlands Fellowship, Abingdon, VA

For years, Pastors around the world have sought new and different ways to effectively preach the gospel of Jesus Christ. There's the traditional and then there's the "not-so-traditional" approaches. Sometimes, even the most "scholared" of ministers has to think outside the box.

Just ask Jimmie Davidson.

The Pastor of Highlands Fellowship in Abingdon, Virginia, had the desire and the dedication to build an effective ministry when he completed seminary. Coming from a traditional Baptist background, he thought he knew all the methods and techniques to fulfill his passion for reaching the world for Christ. But, he's quick to point out that what he thought would work often didn't. In fact, it got to be frustrating.

"The standard methods for ministry just weren't working," he recalls. "God was trying to get my attention. He wanted me to know that there was another way to 'do' church."

That "other way" was the Purpose Driven model introduced by Pastor Rick Warren at Saddleback Church in Southern California. "I really didn't know how to do things differently, but once I saw the five purposes (worship, fellowship, discipleship, ministry and evangelism), it transformed everything we were doing. God showed me that I really didn't have a clue, but through the Purpose Driven model, he opened my eyes to how he wanted us to reach out to our community."

Davidson points out that this is a biblical approach for a new generation and it's effective. He started Highlands Fellowship seven years ago using the Purpose Driven model. Although the town has a population of just 7,000 more than 2,000 people regularly attend the church. Some come from miles around, but most are locals who have discovered a new way to worship and share the gospel of Jesus Christ.

"People who may not have gone to church for years come and when they leave, they often say, 'I don't know what it is, but if I was to 'do' church this is how I'd do it," he said. "This new approach worked for Saddleback and it's worked for us here."

A key element of the Purpose Driven church model is the ability to adapt and change. Long a believer is the effectiveness of small groups to a church's health and growth, Davidson and his team were preparing "the mother of all connections" for the recent 40 Days of Purpose campaign http://www.purposedriven.com/content.aspx?id=264 , when he received a call from Pastor Brett Eastman (who served as the champion of Small Groups at Saddleback Church for the last five years. He asked us to consider changing our plans and try a new approach - the concept of 'host homes.'"

Davidson explains that for many, the title "small group leader" was a bit scary and intimidating. Saddleback was inviting people to become "host homes" for the campaign and Eastman was asking other churches to do the same.

"We were overwhelmed by the response," he says enthusiastically. "Our dream was to have 1,400 sign up for the program and we ended up with more than 1,600 people in 160 small groups. The sheer number of people who experienced life change during the 40 Days campaign was incredible. It was 1,000 times greater that we ever could have expected."

The "de-centralized" nature of the host-home model allowed everyone in the group to contribute and participate. Each person has something to contribute, not unlike the church body as a whole that Jesus talks about in the New Testament, Davidson points out.

The Pastor proudly talks about one woman in the congregation who had never been in a small group before. She stepped out and took a risk by joining a group. God worked within her and helped to make her into a leader in the group. "People who thought they couldn't be used are being used by God in our church every day. It's amazing," Davidson says. Now the entire church is going through the Doing Lifetogether series and building a deeper understanding of the five purposes for everyone's life. Davidson said, "The best way I know our people can experience the Purpose Driven™ Life is by Doing LifeTogether."

He concluded by pointing out, "We needed to be in smaller groups as a church. The Purpose Driven approach was not only fit for us, but it worked beautifully and our small group ministry, in addition to others is more healthy than ever. Every success that we had has helped us to build and grow."

CASE STUDY: THE SADDLEBACK SMALL GROUP STORY (INTERVIEW WITH BRETT)

Brett Eastman: Former Small Group Champion Saddleback Church

1. **So Brett, you landed at Saddleback Church after serving as the small group champion at Willow Creek for 5 years, how did it all begin?**

    I can remember it like it was yesterday. I was only on staff at Saddleback Church for a few weeks and Rick told me he reserved seats for over 800 men on 7 different 747's headed for Washington, DC for the Promise Keeper Event. I had the bright idea of suggesting we recruit leaders from some of the existing men's groups to launch a few more men's groups from the 800+ men going to the event. Over 300 men said they wanted to join a group and I had a half dozen men to lead them…the story of a small group pastors life.

    I showed up Saturday morning along with everyone else to get into a group and I had a momentary (some would say that's typical) loss of my memory capacity and I tied something that has affectionately come to be called the "Small Group Connection" process. People gather into pairs, then fours, and then groups of eight according to their respective geographical areas. The process simply allows people to traverse down a spiral of questions and the group moves from icebreaker like questions into deeper spiritual conversation. This allows them to discern the relative spiritual shepherd (not leader) in the circle.

    This model follows the Acts 6 example where the disciples encouraged the people "select amongst this church" 7 people to serve tables. We would never tell them that Stephen was later raised up and died a brutal death…Just thought that was too much detail.

2. **This sounds wild. How did it work?**

    Consistent with my life verse…exceedingly abundantly beyond what "I" ever asked or thought! We launched 32 groups that day with almost 300 people connected. We saw some disasters but we also had a seed of an idea that helped to serve the church wide small group campaigns for years to come. We had a 50% group success rate that grew to 72% over and over again until we had connected almost 800 people in groups over a 2 1/2 year period. No longer did we need to raise up the leaders in the moment but we were now seeding the table and living rooms of every ministry with pre qualified leaders.

    We refined the process with training, coaching, raising up not apprentices but co-leaders and the big addition to this was the alignment with the weekend services. We added what we called the "Rick Factor". The secret weapon in any church for recruiting new leaders is and always will be the Senior Pastor.! In one weekend we signed up over 1500 people to get into a group. We learned one of the biggest lessons about the future…Weekend alignment was big…VERY BIG!

3. **Now it sounds like you are talking about 40 Days of Purpose.**
   Rick agreed to video tape himself teaching a bible study on the book of James. The congregation loved it. Finally ordinary members could be leaders because they didn't need the same skills for teaching, facilitation and knowledge of the scripture as Rick had. The only complaint was if Rick was ever going to change his shirt (because we shoot the entire series in one day).

   So we had the number one recruiter on our side, video curriculum, small group and service alignment but we still had only 50% of average weekend attendance connected in a group. Much progress had been made, but we still had 8-12 thousand people to go before we felt like we were fulfilling what God had called us to do. Connect the entire congregation under the care of a shepherd. Then a new idea came to us on the eve of the 40 Days Campaign at Saddleback.

4. **So you connected 50% of your congregation in less than 3 years using the connection strategy, video curriculum, and weekend alignment, but how did you connect 15,000 more adults during 40 Days?**
   When I first came to Saddleback I termed recruiting "host houses" with a simple bible study that Lyman Coleman had given me. Great idea, but its time had not come yet. With the new video curriculum we were able to simply say "If you have a VCR you can be a star". Come on anybody can host a group like this! And they did – 3000+ people opened their homes for 6-8 weeks. I was half overjoyed and half overwhelmed all in the same breath! The elders and myself included thought these people must be living in their cars. I was never more scared to do a little research survey in my life. How long had those people been Christians? In a small group? Or even attended our church?

5. **I'll bet the elders were ready to fire you and call it a day…**
   They probably should have but this was a defining moment for Saddleback Church. Glen Kruen and Tom Holladay helped me create a survey that showed us substantially something big had happened. The research survey said….they were Christians for 14+ years on average, had attended Saddleback for 10+ years and many had attended small groups before. They had heard on average over 500 of Rick Warren's messages. I'd say they were ready to host a video led study and launch a few questions. When all

the dust had settled – Our team trained over 2000+ new hosts and launched another 2300 groups and had well over 20,000 people (a good 10-12,000 more than before) going with Rick Warren through a six week study on the Purpose Driven Life. Reading the book in concert with the 40 Days study was alignment not just at a church level or community level but at the level of every Christian in our church family.

6. **Honestly Brett, was this just a Saddleback or mega church deal?**
I thought so too until I had the opportunity to walk with literally 100's of other churches and now we have seen 1000's of churches using our Purpose Driven™ Group curriculum Doing Lifetogether™ not just get a "taste of the purposes" through 40 Days but be transformed by the purposes using this One Year of Purpose curriculum.. I've yet to meet a church or even a small group that wasn't impacted by the 40 Day campaign. But Day 41 can be very traumatic if the church small group leadership is not prepared for what's next.

7. **So what are some of the key learnings through this process?**
   a. You can launch a small group ministry overnight during a small group campaign but sustaining those groups and developing those leaders is a whole other issue. Just in time leadership training integrated into the DVD and video curriculum is the best way to deliver your training.

   For example, how do you train and develop 1000's of new leaders? Not in a classroom that's for sure. We simply did orientation training for new hosts but we put our basic leader training in a decentralized off campus "just in time" format. Every week you get another 20 minutes of training just when you need it.

   b. The intentional development of a "small group supervision system" is key to retaining them. Not the traditional "coaching" model. A community leader (leader of leaders) is the role in a bi-vocational capacity and it creates shock absorption for the new and existing leaders in the trenches.

   c. At the end of the day – curriculum is the key. It's the factor for both starting and sustaining groups after a campaign. But what to use, when to use it and how to introduce it to your groups is more than important. It's make or break it for up to 50% of your groups. Especially after a campaign, during the fall launch season, and especially what you communicate in your leadership training and weekend series.

   d. Finally recruiting unlimited leaders really is possible in any church anytime of the year. But especially late September, January and after Easter. The problem is most Pastors and church leaders think in terms of 40 days, just for the fall or for a sermon series.

   How do you recruit unlimited leaders to lead these groups? You got to grow your own like we did back in the 60"s. Leaders are best trained and developed in the living rooms of Life than in my little six week or 16 week training class that

I used to think was the reason our groups did so well in the past. I'm ashamed to admit it now but when we launched 200 new groups and it was just me and nor coaches I thought I will train them all in this ½ day class. They all came but I didn't have one coach, division leader or infrastructure in place. Well over a year later 80% plus were still rolling along. Can I really say it was my little 2-3 hour class? Forgive me Lord and shame on anybody else who tries to take credit for it.

8. **Brett, it sounds like it worked, but where was it messy?**
Please don't misunderstand me I have had my share of blow ups like the guy who told me he and his live-in girlfriend were so excited about the 20 people they coming to their group. Or the member who called me and said is it OK to be studying the new book "Embracing the Light" instead of a bible study? But these honestly are the exception not the rule. And by the way I just married that couple above, a few weeks later in a break out room at Saddleback filled with their small group cheering them on, and them being the most mature of their seeker group we let them carry on given their recent act of obedience when they were confronted with the truth. You should have seen the baptism that day with over 10 of those seekers being baptized by their relative spiritual shepherd… Sorry I just couldn't let that go.

The bottom line is you have to ask a very basic question at this point…"what is the point of 40 Days of Purpose? Or any spiritual or small group campaign for that matter? It's simply organizing principle, program & process – to help the people in the church live healthy balanced Purpose Driven™ Lives. Not just about connecting people into community for the sake of community, but changing community through community in order to convert our culture for the sake of Christ. Because that's what he came to do…not just the upper room but the bottom of the cross so that we might do our lives together with Him and one another.

CASE STUDY
HOW ONE CHURCH PLANTED OVER 100 PURPOSE-DRIVEN CHURCHES

New Life Christian Center, Turlock, California

As a child, I was indoctrinated in a heresy that has crippled many churches for years. Our Sunday School teacher had us interlock our fingers and close our hands, then recite this mantra, "Here is the church. Here is the steeple. Go inside and see all the people." It was confusing enough that our church building did not actually have a steeple. But, any talk of the "early church" sounded like something that inspectors should have condemned long ago.

Most of us have come to accept that the church is a group of believers committed to fulfilling the Great Commandment and the Great Commission. These commands of Jesus give us the basis of the Purpose-Driven church. Whether you have a church building or a rented facility, each gathering of believers constitutes a church. If we accept that, well, we're half right.

The early church met in the temple courts (which we get) as well as meeting house to house (Acts 2:46). Many pastors will protest at this point and say, "But, we have small groups." But, what do your small groups look like?

Some churches encourage fellowship groups. Believers are encouraged to gather together just to get to know each other, to spend social time together, and maybe to even pray for needs. Groups are discouraged from opening their Bibles or getting into a theological discussion. Their pastors want them to leave the Bible teaching to the experts. But, they do see the value in members growing deeper in their relationships. After all, if members are better connected to each other, then they'll also be better connected to the church (or they'll leave the church in groups rather than individually—sorry to raise that fear).

While fellowship is one of the biblical purposes of the church, it is not the only purpose that groups can fulfill. Many churches encourage their groups in fellowship and discipleship. Groups gather to get to know each other and to study God's Word. While this requires a more skilled group leader or the help of DVD-based curriculum, groups can fulfill two out of five purposes. I believe that there is great potential when believers who are filled with the Spirit of God interact with the Word of God. The problem is that these groups often become very devoted to each other and their own spiritual growth, but do not consider their place in serving and influencing others outside of the fold.

If you consider the DNA of the early church (Acts 2:42-46), you will see that they devoted themselves to fellowship (Acts 2:46), discipleship (Acts 2:42), ministry (Acts 2:43-45), worship (Acts 2: 42, 46) and evangelism (Acts 2:47). These purposes were demonstrated in both large and small formats (temple courts and house to house). What I am getting at is simply this: healthy small groups are actually small churches. While fellowship and discipleship are hallmarks of small groups, worship, ministry and evangelism are also key elements of these small churches.

Some argue that worship is done best on Sunday morning with a talented worship team. But something as simple as a worship DVD turn up fairly loud provides a great small group worship experience.

Ministry and evangelism are key elements to any healthy group. I have seen groups of adults who would never step out and serve on their own fall under the wonderful peer pressure of their small group and serve hot meals to the homeless. Groups invite friends and neighbors and see them develop a relationship with Jesus Christ.

Our church, New Life Christian Center, Turlock, California, has been a Purpose-Driven church for 12 years now. When our senior pastor, David Larson, took us to our very first Purpose-Driven Church Conference in the Spring of 1993, we knew that God was calling our church to fulfill these purposes.

What we didn't understand was that God did not want us to limit our activities to building only one church. We saw the benefit of small groups in fleshing out the purpose of fellowship. We also saw the value of small groups focusing on God's Word to encourage discipleship. What we missed is exactly what I've described: creating well-rounded, purpose-driven small churches in our church body.

Think about it. Why would we encourage our members to understand more of God's Word, yet giving the impression that acting on God's Word was merely an option? After all, most of us are already educated way beyond our level of obedience. I've even heard some group members remark that the studies didn't seem very "deep." I said, "Sure, it doesn't seem very deep if you're only talking about it."

Today, it's a different story. Recently, a brand new host asked me if it was okay if she gathered a new group of people who did not attend our church. All I could do was smile and give her a big hug.

Our small groups have taken on the challenge of providing a hot meal to the homeless in our community every Friday night during the Winter months. At the start of our second year of providing meals, our groups filled up the list for every Friday night in one hour. Fridays this year included Christmas Eve and New Year's Eve! My group didn't even have a chance to sign up.

New Life Christian Center is a Purpose-Driven church made up of over 100 Purpose-Driven small churches. Our next goal is to move beyond our three county radius and plant Purpose-Driven small churches throughout the world.

CASE STUDY: BEGINNING LIFETOGETHER (INTERVIEW WITH BRETT)

Joey O'Connor, Coast Hills Church, CA

Brett: Joey is from a church here in Southern California called Coast Hills Community Church. They've been a real popular church in the area. They've been running about 1600 or so last year in the October-November. They didn't do 40 Days but they did a functional 40 Days by using the Beginning Life Together curriculum which is similar to the 40 Days series. The big thing about this is that Joey is a lay guy who ended up jumping in on this stuff. He's the future of what I believe we could do with all the coaching churches. He's stepping up to a very significant role in his church. He's now on part time staff. He's one of those guys that you won't know unless somebody else tells you. He's a gift to the church with a gift of leadership and what God has done. I'll let him tell you. Go ahead, Joey.

Joey: Thanks, Brett. When we started Beginnings Life Together curriculum our history at Coast Hills, Coast Hills has been around about 18 years. At the height of its small group home Bible studies we probably had about 100 groups. That was probably 10 years ago. Before we started the Beginnings Life Together series, this fall we were starting with 35-40 groups out in the community. It's one of our goals as we were building towards this and working with the Life Together consulting team. We were working in the fall and we wanted to reach to have 100 hosts identified before we went public in the Sunday morning services. So our goal by was by the end of December to just do a lot of private asks, a lot of one on one, a lot of coffees with people. So when we reached that goal when we went public in January and 3 weeks of getting hosts and getting people involved we hit 220 host homes throughout south Orange County.

When we added up all the numbers when we met with Brett and Chris a couple weeks ago we found that we had 1500 people participating in the Life Together ministry with the 220 host homes. That represents about 87% of our weekly congregation. So that's been really great. More specifically what we're doing now, the next step we're taking is we're going to be developing community leaders. So that in each of the surrounding communities in talking with Chris and Brett we really want to take the church to the community versus expecting the community to come to church. So we're working to develop 2-3 community letters in each geographic area. And as we're working toward this next round, this next 6 week period using the curriculum we're finding that we're going to be at a 90% retention level of recurrent folks. Also it's important to note that Coast Hills is in a major leadership transition. Our senior pastor has resigned and we're doing a search. So for those of you in churches in times of transition and maybe some struggle, this program, this ministry really does work because it's simple, it's transferable, it's low maintenance but highly relational program.

CASE STUDY: SMALL TOWN, BIG IMPACT

Dave Holden, Lake Gregory Community Church

My name is Dave Holden. I'm pastor of Lake Gregory Community church. We're in southern California. We're half way between Los Angeles and Palm Springs. It's a mountain community. We've got one zip code, 80,000 people. When we started our purpose driven process there was 150 of us. Now we're pushing 1000 every Sunday. That's pretty good in a small town. But the thing that excited us is I was challenged by Brett. He came alongside of me. He gave me a challenge to increase my small groups. I was one of those guys who always wanted a small group ministry. I believed in it. But the most I could do was get 7 groups. With 40 Days of Purpose and utilizing a host program that Brett dreamed up, by using this video curriculum, we went from 7 small groups to 72 small groups and I have retained close to 60. I think there's 58 at this time. So what we've learned is, is that by continuing in community with other leaders particularly my relationship with Brett, has kept me going kept me learning. I have a small volunteer staff now. We meet every week and we ask ourselves what can we do next with small groups. What we're looking forward to is we've created a table/ booth where all of our small group leaders can come on a weekly basis, pick up new materials. We've pretty much devoted ourselves to the Life Together material because it's step by step and it's all Purpose Driven. But we're just going crazy right now with small groups. And the leaders are coming out of the woodwork. Simultaneously I'm not doing a lot of begging and God makes me so happy I hate to beg. So there's my story.

I'm in a little mountain town called Crestline. We're near Lake Arrowhead. Maybe you've heard of that. It's about halfway between Los Angeles California and Palm Springs. So we're kind of in the shadow of Saddleback Community Church, about an hour and a half from them. If that gives you an idea of where we're at. There's about 8500 people in my town. We have one zip code so it's definitely a small town. We're surrounded by national forests and God has really done some neat things with us just helping our church to grow. One of the wildest rides we have ever been on was with the 40 Days of Purpose and especially launching and now maintain in a really vital small group network. What happened was in all the years I've been here about 11 years I had been here I had really never been able to cultivate more than 7 groups. I was invited by Brett Eastman to participate in a learning cycle of what it would take to grow small groups and maintain them and keep them healthy and vital. I came back home and in the middle of 40 days of purpose we had already started I began to implement some of Brett's great ideas. One of them was just the host home idea. Host was a very simple acronym. It meant H – stands for do you have a Heart for this church? Do you love this church? O – will you be willing to Open up your home. S – We said Will you Serve some snacks? And T – We said will you take the Time to recruit people to come to your home for the next 6 weeks?

People responded like crazy. It went from 7 small groups which that was all we had ever had all the way to 72 groups. That meant every adult had a place to go. At the end of the 40 Days I was expecting a real drop off in the groups but it did not come. Right now we're still maintaining somewhere between 50-55 groups. That is quite a change from 7. What we're hoping to do as we continue on in relationships with other people just like you that are interested in small groups is the coaching that made all the difference in the world for us here at Lake Gregory. If I hadn't had someone to come alongside of me and give me a next step I'm not sure I would have ever taken that step. After the 40 Days what happened for a number of weeks, in fact a number of months we were on the telephone together with a group of guys from all over the place in a conference call just like this and in community all around this topic of small group we began talking together and heading off problems guys had experienced and they were experimenting with new things. We were able to pick up where other guys had left off. I believe that that's why our small groups are as strong as they are today. So I can't say enough about just getting together with guys like you and growing a healthy small group ministry. It comes through this kind of community and the coaching that we have through Life Together. So anyway, that's a little bit of my story. I hope that that was good.

We've got one zip code 92325. One of the big restaurants in town used to be the A&W. You'd be able to pull up and get that. But they couldn't sell enough root beer so they took their franchise and they had to take one of the letters off so now we just call it the "A". That's the size of my town. There's 8500 of us in this town. On any given Sunday morning right now we're running about 950 every Sunday. When this really started taking off for us was when I got together and I got some coaching behind the scenes from Brett. Brett had encouraged me to try something called the Host program. Just while we launched 40 Days of Purpose. What HOST stood for was – you just ask people right in the church services. That's the way I did it. I said, "Do you have a Heart for our church? O – Would you Open your home? S – Would you Serve some snacks? And T – would you take the Time to get your own people because I couldn't possibly recruit everybody." We had never had more than 7 small groups. At that point we went from 7 to 72. That happened within a 2 week period. I've been able to retain about 55 of those groups. We have a push all the time for new leaders. But we're using the DVD curriculum so that people don't feel like they have to go out there and give their life to it every week. But what they do is they study that DVD. It takes them a few moments. They know what's going to happen. There are groups that just keep going on and on and on. I think the secret that I've discovered is that to have someone that's coaching you and encouraging you as part of a small group community has really been helpful. I've been able to be on the phone with Brett and guys like Chris throughout this last year. I think that's what keeps us going and going strong. So when we went into 40 Days we had about 93% of our adults in small groups. Now what I'm looking forward to with ongoing coaching as being a part of our small group community is learning how to take it from 100%. Because I cannot tell you what it does for your church. Everybody's healthy, happy, connected and things really take off. So Chris I hope that was…

Chris: That was great Dave. I really appreciate that. That's an amazing testimony in a town of 8500. You started out around 200 didn't you?

Dave: Actually I'm not bragging here but we started out at 150. That was after 70 years of being a church. Now we're hitting 950 a week.

CASE STUDY: CONNECTING EVERYONE

Pastor Scott Mawdesley, Christ Fellowship in West Palm Beach Florida

Before we get back to Brett, he asked me if I would share a brief testimony for about a minute of what God has done here at Christ Fellowship. We are located in West Palm Beach Florida. A year ago we did not have a small group ministry. We did not even have a Sunday school. We were basically high on programs and low on process. Through connecting with Brett and launching the 40 Days of Purpose almost a year and a half ago now God just created a fire in our church where people came out of the 40 Days of Purpose saying, What's next? What's going on for Day 41? So we got connected with Brett and Brett kind of threw out this idea of this hosting strategy with DVD driven video curriculum. So we just went for it. We recruited hosts. We recruited participants. In a matter of 6 weeks we were able to launch about 300 groups with about 3000 people – in a matter of 6 weeks. Needless to say it's been quite a ride.

In the past year we have found that not only people for the first time are getting connected in community and finding a place where they're actually cared for amidst the thousands of people. Right now we have an average of about 9000 people on the weekend. Most of you know that even when you come into a congregation of a couple hundred, it's tough to get connected to people and get to know each other. But what we've found is that our people not only have a place to connect now but this whole hosting strategy that we've done has allowed us to find leadership left and right that we didn't even know were sitting out in our congregation. Many of them have been in our church for 3 or 4 years and for the first time they've found something that they could do, a place they could plug in. So for us it's been an unbelievable ride. Right now we're still sitting with about 230 some odd groups with over 2500 people in small groups. We're well on our way to creating a culture of discipleship in small groups. There's a lot more I could say about that. But this whole strategy that Brett's going to be talking with you about today is something that has revolutionized our church here at Christ Fellowship. His added component that we did not have that has allowed us to connect for us thousands of people at one time that would have never been able to be connected otherwise.

A 'BLOCKBUSTER' SMALL GROUP STRATEGY

by Brett Eastman

When was the last time you watched a movie at home with your family and a few friends? Did you call the church office to decide whose house you would go to? Did you ask your pastor who to invite?

Probably not!

If you are like most people, you just drove over to your local video store, checked out a movie, and called a friend or two. If that's the case for most Christians, then why do we go to so much trouble signing people up to get into small groups and matching them with a small group leader?

Do we not trust them to invite the "right" people? To turn on a DVD or VCR? Or do our church attendees and members not have any friends, family, neighbors or co-workers they would like to hang out with for a few weeks studying a DVD-driven Bible study?

I realize this may be a new idea, but ironically it better follows Jesus' model for forming his own small group community with the 12 disciples. First he spent time with a number of "Christ followers" getting to know them and discerning whether they would be the ones he "asked" to join his own group. Then the Bible says he prayed overnight to confirm if they were the ones, and then the next day he simply asked them to come with him.

The model followed a simple A-B-C plan to create your own community and to not do your life alone but to do life together in community with a few other friends and family.

Discover the ABCs of Jesus' small group strategy:

Ask God who he wants you or even is calling you to connect with. Reflect on the fact that this is not about a 40 Day journey but a simple but intentional step. God, from the model of the Trinity, to the way he modeled ministry through Jesus, showed us it was a healthy balance of alone to pray and meditate but also a clear call to not do ministry alone but to do ministry and life together!

Practically, a senior pastor delivers a message on community on a Sunday morning to set up the vision, asking everyone to follow Jesus' model of doing life together. Whether it's 40 Days of Purpose, 40 Days of Community, or any other curriculum series, the formula is the same.

The first approach is to say, "Think about your lists in life." An obvious one is your cell phone list. Ask them -- for the first time in the church's life -- to turn on their cell phones and look at their contact list. Have them scroll through and pick up a few names. What about their address list at home on the Christmas card list, sports team list, PTA list, neighborhood list, school list, on and on?

BUILDINGLIFE**TOGETHER**

Take these lists and have your congregation consider who they would enjoy getting together with for just six weeks. Have them start a list right there in the service! After a moment of prayerful reflection, challenge them by asking, "Would you follow Jesus' model?" People respond out of obedience, out of a longing to belong, or a desire to help the pastor and their church reach out and extend the circle to a few others. Don't make this about the cause as much as about the "call to community."

Begin calling the names of the 3-5-8-12 names God gave you. The beauty of this model is that it's not a matter of if, it's a matter of *when* you are going to do it and who you're going to call. You've taken care of the if by saying you want to grow like Jesus did. That brings us to the question of when. If everybody's doing a campaign that kicks off in two weeks, you have two weeks to promote this on the weekend.

Trust me on this one, if you give them a message on the value of community from any message in your files, you will be amazed by what happens. Simply say, "All I'm asking you to do is be willing to call the names that God just gave you in the next 24 to 36 hours." You minimize the "ask" in order to maximize the response. Say to them, "Come on. You can put up with anyone for just six weeks -- many of you have spouses that have to live with you for a lifetime."

Challenge them to go home and call two or three people today! Most people will at least get one yes within 24 hours, and then they are committed. Remind them that these groups don't have be big, they just need to begin with a man or woman of faith -- not seminary professors or pastors, just a few friends. The Scripture says "Where two or more are gathered (not 22 or even 12 like Jesus)."

Have them turn in names they write down on their pages, collect them, and then have the staff pray for them during the week. This will show you are in this with them. You can't ask them to do something you're not willing to do. When you have a day of fasting and prayer for those names, it will be one of the most emotional days your staff has ever had.

Check out the curriculum they can use for the six weeks series. Whether you do sermon alignment or not, still challenge them to pick up a sampler a (DVD/VCR and study guide) as they walk out of the service today. One church put the material in gift bags and had people come up front, like an altar call. In a church of 1,600, they handed out 220 DVD/study guide sampler kits. I went to this church the next weekend and trained over 250 hosts/leaders.

For those pastors and church leaders reading this, let me just say, "You can do this!" And it's possible to do it over the next few weeks. Any one of the Purpose Driven™ six-week curriculum series would work. I just suggest a sermon alignment either before Easter or after Easter.

You might want to use one of the ministry or evangelism series (Rick Warren's or Doing Life Together) before Easter to prepare your congregation for the after-Easter assimilation series.

After Easter, I recommend any "open" curriculum series on fellowship, discipleship themes, or typical series like John Ortberg's or Phillip Yancy's six-session DVD series.

For those who want to focus on the Easter theme, the three week Purpose Driven Passion series would also be an excellent choice either before or after Easter along with the Experiencing Christ Together series by Lifetogether.

My experience with this "blockbuster" idea is that more than 20% of adults will do this if the senior pastor or small group champion simply stands up and challenges the congregation to go for it. This can be done in the middle of a message and illustrated by a testimony or two.

What percentage of your adults do you think will respond to a call that came out of a message casting vision for whatever campaign using whatever series you are going to do? I have asked this question to senior pastors and church leaders for almost a year, the number is always between 50% and 75%.

If you do a good job casting Jesus' vision and talk about the value of community, the benefits of community you will be amazed.

RICK WARRREN FOREWORD FOR DOING LIFETOGETHER

A Puprose Driven Group Resource

Doing Life Together is a groundbreaking study in several ways. It is the first small group curriculum built completely on the purpose-driven paradigm. This is not just another study to be used in your church; it is a study on the church to help strengthenyour church. Many small group curricula today are quite self-focused and individualistic. They generally do not address the importance of the local church and our role in it as believers. Another unique feature of this curriculum is its balance. In every session, the five purposes of God are stressed in some way.

But the greatest reason I am excited about releasing this Doing Life Together curriculum is that I've seen the dramatic changes it produces in the lives of those who study it. These small group studies were not developed in some detached ivory tower or academic setting but in the day-to-day ministry of Saddleback Church, where thousands of people meet weekly in small groups that are committed to fulfilling God's purposes. This curriculum has been tested and retested, and the results have been absolutely amazing. Lives have been changed, marriages saved, and families strengthened. And our church has grown-in the past seven years we've seen over 9,100 new believers baptized at Saddleback. I attribute these results to the fact that so many of our members are serious about living healthy, balanced, purpose-driven lives.

It is with great joy and expectation that I introduce this resource to you. I am so proud of our development team on this project: Brett and Dee Eastman, Todd and Denise Wendorff, and Karen Lee-Thorp. They have committed hundreds of hours to write, teach, develop, and refine these lessons - with much feedback along the way. This has been a labor of love, as they have shared our dream of helping you serve God's purpose in your own generation. The church will be enriched for eternity as a result.

Get ready for a life-changing journey. God bless! - Pastor Rick Warren

DOING LIFETOGETHER SERIES

Lifetogether Small Group Curriculum Series

Doing Lifetogether—Purpose Driven Group Series
* Student Edition of all 6 studies also available
- Beginning Lifetogether (God's Purpose for Your Life)
- Connecting with God's Family (Fellowship)
- Growing to Be Like Christ (Discipleship)
- Developing Your SHAPE to Serve Others (Ministry)
- Sharing Your Life Mission Every Day (Evangelism)
- Surrendering Your Life to God's Pleasure (Worship)

Experiencing Christ Together
* Student Edition of all 6 also available

- Beginning in Christ Together (Life of Jesus)
- Connecting in Christ Together (Fellowship)
- Growing in Christ Together (Discipleship)
- Serving Like Christ Together (Ministry)
- Sharing Christ Together (Evangelism)
- Surrendering to Christ Together (Worship)

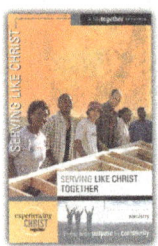

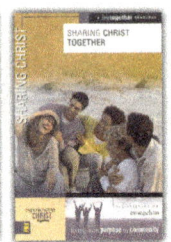

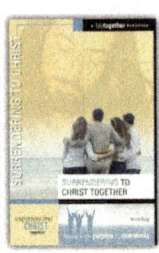

Deepening Lifetogether (8 Individual Studies)
Building Character Together (6 Individual Studies)

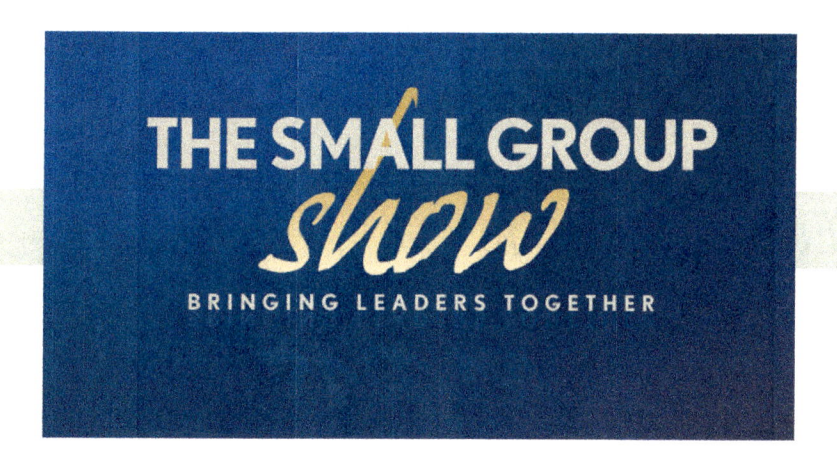

WELCOME TO THE SMALL GROUP SHOW
Hosted by Brett Eastman and Steve Gladen

The Small Group Show is a free resource distributed to small group ministry leaders, pastors and champions across the country. We are interviewing some of the best, the most influential, and interesting men and women in the small group movement today in a talk show format to help encourage and inform local small group workers.

The show is built on 6 T's:

Testimony: A guest shares a piece of his or her testimony as it relates to small groups, from joining a group, to becoming a leader, pastor or director in order to others on the same journey.

Training: This segment features training on a myriad of different topics related to small groups. It will give you new ideas, wisdom and tools to more effectively start and sustain a small group ministry

Together: This segment highlights small group conferences and other larger training opportunities around the country

Tip of the Week: Our guests share advice on what could be a simple key to improving a small group, or small group ministry.

Tool: Our guests discuss books they have written, blogs they are reading, podcasts they listen to and other resources that will help you and your small group ministry.

Trend: We discuss what is new and next with our guests. How they see small group ministry evolving and tell you how to stay on the cutting edge.

Sign up to receive the Small Group Show at Lifetogether.com

SMALL GROUP UNIVERSITY

BUILDINGLIFETOGETHER

Building Leaders for Life

building leaders for life

This breakthrough small group training course is the first DVD-based training system designed by Brett Eastman, the creator of the award winning Purpose-Driven TM Small Group resource Doing Lifetogether. Small Group University provides the next level in building healthy small groups that build healthy Christians over time.

Small Group University provides a proven pathway to train new and existing small group leaders in any size church at any stage of their small group ministry. **Hosting Lifetogether** helps anyone "create their own community" with a few of their friends and family. **Coaching Lifetogether** gives practical training to your experienced leaders and coaches. **Building Lifetogether** gives practical and proven support to pastors and small group directors in building and growing a small group ministry. Best of all, it provides pastors with everything they need to launch and lead a healthy small group ministry in their churches in less than 90 days.

Hosting Lifetogether - Creating Your Own Community

This 6-session DVD and companion study guide will provide the initial or in service small group leader/host training based on the 5 purposes. This series is perfect for new hosts training either in a classroom, coaching huddle or self paced online study. The package includes six video teaching sessions on DVD based on the five purposes, personal testimonies, and inspirational stories for your leaders to study on a daily basis.

Coaching Lifetogether - Creating Healthy Leaders and Their Members

The **Coaching Lifetogether** Training Series is the first DVD training series of its kind designed for experienced leaders and emerging small group coaches and community leaders in your church. This series will help recruit, train, and develop your leaders of leaders! This series shares proven strategies and transforming principles straight from the front lines of ministry. You can develop a group of well-trained coaches who cultivate healthy groups that produce purpose driven lives over time. You will learn timely methods to apply timeless truths of coaching your new and existing small group leaders and their small groups. The 6 lesson series comes complete on DVD and CD and includes a 150 page comprehensive training handbooks.

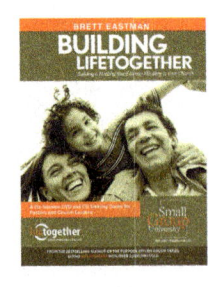

Building Lifetogether - Creating a Healthy Small Group Ministry at Your Church

The Building Lifetogether Training Series is designed for a senior pastor, church leader, or volunteer small group champion helping to launch and lead a healthy small group ministry in your church. This 6-lesson series provides practical how-to's for starting and sustaining your small groups. Whether you are trying to sustain the new groups you have recently begun or trying to multiply your existing small groups, Building Lifetogether will become your personal coach on how to get there. The 6 lessons come on both DVD and CD with 170-page training handbook.

ABOUT THE AUTHOR

Brett Eastman served as the Small Group Champion at Saddleback Church and Willow Creek Community Church for over a decade. Brett has produced and either authored or co-authored over 200 small group curriculum series including the bestselling Purpose Driven Small Group curriculum, *Doing Lifetogether* published by Zondervan, which has sold over 3,000,000 copies. He also was the primary designer behind the 40 Days of Purpose Campaigns that fueled over 25,000 churches around the world. He also wrote and produced the first Purpose Driven small group series for Rick Warren that influenced the development of over 50 small group series to date.

Brett received a B.A. in Marketing from San Diego State University. He then worked in technology and training in the Silicon Valley, partnering with companies like Apple, Xerox and Novell. He later earned his Masters of Divinity degree from the graduate school of Biola University, Talbot School of Theology and received a Management Certificate from Kellogg School of Management at Northwestern University in Chicago, Illinois.

In 1989 Brett founded Lifetogether, a ministry committed to championing the small group movement around the world. Brett has produced award-winning resources for the top 100 Churches and Christian Ministries Today. Some of the publishing partners include Zondervan, Tyndale, Baker Books, Thomas Nelson, Focus on the Family, *Christianity Today,* Serendipity, Purpose Driven Ministries, David C. Cook, just to name a few.

Dee Eastman is the real hero in the family, who, after giving birth to Joshua and Breanna, gave birth to identical triplet girls—Meagan, Melody, and Michelle. Dee is the Director of the Daniel Plan at Saddleback Church and co-leader "The Journey" a women's Bible Study at Saddleback Church. The Eastman's live in Las Flores, California.

152 **BUILDING**LIFE**TOGETHER**

TANYA KAY
PHOTOGRAPHY

tanyakayphoto.com

Multiple pictures are provided by Tanya Kay Photography. Her images have been featured in local and international publications. She specializes in wedding, portrait, fashion, and photojournalism.

Inspired by her faith, she strives to use her lens to capture hope. An advocate for the hurting and the broken, she uses her gift as a contributing artist for Unseen Ministries, a global team of artists who bring freedom, truth, and love to the unknown.

UNSEEN MINISTRIES

www.unseenministries.net

PRAYER AND PRAISE REPORT

Briefly share your prayer requests with the large group, making notations below. Then gather in small groups of two, three, or four to pray for each need.

PRAYER REQUEST	PRIASE REPORT

PRAYER AND PRAISE REPORT

PRAYER REQUEST	PRIASE REPORT